Praise for Refresh

'Caroline Montgomery is a person of spiritual vision and practical wisdom, and writes with an engaging and accessible style. As the local bishop for the church where Refresh began, I saw how it proved a fruitful and effective way for the church to offer physical, emotional and spiritual refreshment to young families in the local area. Reinventing wheels is rarely a worthwhile exercise, and so for anyone looking to do something similar, this book provides an easily replicable and adaptable model, and I commend it highly.'
Rt Revd Dr Graham Tomlin, director of the Centre for Cultural Witness

'The Refresh model is simple to implement yet highly effective. As people get hold of this practical guide and start using it in their community, I expect to see hundreds of lives transformed. Caroline has done all the hard work of pioneering and honing the model, to cover everything that you need to know and set you up for success.'
Anna Hawken, Parenting for Faith ministry lead

'Refresh is a fantastic resource that helps introduce a spiritual edge to church toddler groups and provides a natural discipleship pathway into the heart of the church. This is ready to use, accessible and packed with insights, forged by Caroline's experience of doing the hard work for us. It is just what the church needs today.'
Rt Revd Dr Ric Thorpe, Bishop of Islington

'A warm, inspiring and practical guide to a simple and effective way that churches can welcome and support parents and carers.'
Helen Lock, Playtime Coordinator, Care for the Family

BRF

15 The Chambers, Vineyard
Abingdon OX14 3FE
brf.org.uk

Bible Reading Fellowship is a charity (233280)
and company limited by guarantee (301324),
registered in England and Wales

ISBN 978 1 80039 216 8
First published 2023
10 9 8 7 6 5 4 3 2 1 0
All rights reserved

Text © Caroline Montgomery 2023
This edition © Bible Reading Fellowship 2023
Cover image © somemeans/stock.adobe.com, Rawpixel.com/stock.adobe.com

The author asserts the moral right to be identified as the author of this work

Acknowledgements

Unless otherwise acknowledged, scripture quotations are taken from The Holy Bible, New International Version®, NIV® Copyright © 1973, 1978, 1984, 2011 by Biblica, Inc.® Used by permission. All rights reserved worldwide.

Scripture quotations marked TPT are taken from The Passion Translation®. Copyright © 2017, 2018, 2020 by Passion & Fire Ministries, Inc. Used by permission. All rights reserved. thePassionTranslation.com. Scripture quotations marked GNT are taken from the Good News Bible published by The Bible Societies/HarperCollins Publishers Ltd, UK © American Bible Society 1966, 1971, 1976, 1992, used with permission. Scripture quotations marked NLT are taken from The Holy Bible, New Living Translation, copyright © 1996, 2004, 2007, 2013. Used by permission of Tyndale House Publishers, Inc., Carol Stream, Illinois 60188. All rights reserved. Scripture quotations marked ESV are taken from The Holy Bible, English Standard Version, published by HarperCollins Publishers, © 2001 Crossway Bibles, a division of Good News Publishers. Used by permission. All rights reserved. Scripture quotations marked MSG are taken from *The Message*, copyright © 1993, 1994, 1995, 1996, 2000, 2001, 2002 by Eugene H. Peterson. Used by permission of NavPress. All rights reserved. Represented by Tyndale House Publishers, Inc.

Some names and places have been changed.

Every effort has been made to trace and contact copyright owners for material used in this resource. We apologise for any inadvertent omissions or errors, and would ask those concerned to contact us so that full acknowledgement can be made in the future.

A catalogue record for this book is available from the British Library

Printed and bound by CPI Group (UK) Ltd, Croydon CR0 4YY

Refresh

Introducing adults
to faith through
toddler groups

Caroline Montgomery

BRF

Contents

Introduction 7

Part I - About Refresh

1   The vision for Refresh 10

2   What Refresh looks like: practicalities and details 19

3   Team recruiting, regulations and roles 30

4   Testimonies and stories 37

Part II - Thoughts for the day

5   The thought for the day: what it is and how to do it 50

6   33 thoughts for the day for you to use 56
    Beginning of term 59
    Priorities 61
    Encouragement 63
    Different seasons and stages of life 73
    God loves us 78
    God helps us 89
    We can make a difference 95
    Hope 103
    Special occasions 107
    End of the summer term 112
    Other ideas and tips 114

Appendix 1 Refresh layout – diagrams of the setup 115

Appendix 2 Preparation to do in advance and on the day 117

Appendix 3 List of toys we use and playdough recipe 118

Appendix 4 Registration table list and sample register 120

Appendix 5 Examples of Bible verses with pictures 122

Appendix 6 Index of Bible verses 124

Acknowledgements

Thank you to all who have helped pioneer Refresh, those who prayed at the beginning and have continued to pray, especially Elaine Johnston and those who joined the team and contributed so much over the years (35 in total!) – you have been such a blessing to so many people, including me! Particular thanks to those who have written some of the thoughts for the day in this book: Amy Baird, Helen Chen and Sarah Mumford. And thanks too to Jez Barnes, the vicar of St Stephen's, for his support and to the staff there, especially Victoria Byrne for her book-writing advice. To Janet Tomlin for reading everything through, and of course, to my long-suffering husband Richard for his patience and encouragement.

Photocopying for churches

Please report to CLA Church Licence any photocopy you make from this publication. Your church administrator or secretary will know who manages your CLA Church Licence.

The information you need to provide to your CLA Church Licence administrator is as follows:

Title, Author, Publisher and ISBN

If your church doesn't hold a CLA Church Licence, information about obtaining one can be found at uk.ccli.com

Introduction

Refresh is a fun and effective way to build meaningful and purposeful relationships with parents and carers in your community. It's stay-and-play turned on its head; the children have fun, but we focus on refreshing the adults with time to talk, fresh coffee, pastries and, most importantly, our key ingredient: a five-minute thought for the day where we share something of God in a gentle, relevant and accessible way. The adults feel like it's *their* morning: a place where they are welcomed, encouraged and refreshed, that is also fun for their little ones. Our guests include parents, carers, grandparents, nannies and childminders.

I'm pleased to be writing this book because Refresh has been such a blessing to the families in our community and we have had the joy of journeying alongside many who have now found Jesus for themselves. I am excited to share all about it with you and give you the resources to run your own Refresh!

The Refresh model is straightforward and proven to work. It could be used in a large or small setting; the model works regardless of size. I would encourage you to try it in your setting, it is such a joy to see how God meets with the parents and carers in the community. We have seen much fruit from our Refresh Café. Families who previously were not part of church have started coming along on Sundays; many have become Christians, and their journeys all began with Refresh. You can read some testimonies in chapter 4.

There are numerous groups for parents and carers to attend with their little ones, but most, if not all, are completely focused on the children and there is little or nothing offered specifically for the adults. Even those run by churches often centre their activities totally around the children. It is also true that most of the families coming to these groups are from the wider community and are not part of any church. As Christians, we need to find a way to connect with these families, welcome, love and support them and show them that God loves them. We have found Refresh to be an excellent way to do all this.

My heart and purpose for writing this book is to encourage and equip you to grow your own Refresh ministry in your church; to create a space in the week where families are welcomed, where the children are happy and where you can invest in refreshing the adults physically, emotionally and, most importantly, spiritually. You can do this with a five-minute Christian thought for the day that shares something of God with them.

Whatever your church situation and space, I suggest that it is possible to create an environment that is safe and fun for the children, while at the same time operating principally as a welcoming space for the adults. This book shows you how to run Refresh in your setting and includes 33 thoughts for the day for you to use. These can be used straight off the page, or you can adapt them using your own examples and stories, but there are enough to take you through the academic year.

My prayer is that your community will be blessed and strengthened through the transformational love of God and will experience amazing new testimonies of faith such as we have seen through pioneering Refresh Café, in Jesus' name.

About Refresh

1

The vision for Refresh

> It's wonderful to have a morning where the focus is on me being refreshed!
>
> Refresh attendee

Our vision for Refresh was to create a space where families, particularly the adults, would be welcomed, encouraged and refreshed, and where they might experience something of God's love for them in a space that is also suitable and fun for their little ones.

In this chapter I'm going to look at how Refresh came about and the key elements that make up its DNA. I will describe the journey we went on as we felt challenged to move from the more traditional style of church toddler groups, which we had run in the past, to a model which focuses on the adults and is more intentional about connecting with them spiritually.

In the beginning

Our church had a strong history of running well-attended toddler groups, but God began to challenge us to engage with the children's adult carers in a more overtly spiritual way and that led us on a path to start Refresh. This is how Refresh was born.

I was helping at our church's popular and very busy stay-and-play group when during one session, in conversation with a parent, I said something about being part of St Stephen's Church, to which they responded,

'Oh, I hadn't realised this was anything to do with church. I thought this group just used the building!' That comment went right to my spirit; it broke my heart to think that many of our guests came every week but hadn't connected what we offered with Jesus in any way at all. Of course, there were team who shared their stories and significant conversations and friendships grew out of that group. I don't want to dismiss any of those or belittle those experiences, but it challenged me to wonder if there was a way we could be more intentional as a team. Could we have a prevailing atmosphere and climate of being open to spiritual conversations in a way that would be natural and easy to do without it being cringy or difficult for the team if they didn't see themselves as natural evangelists? There is a chapter on team later in the book where I will unpack this more and look at the variety of roles that team members can play.

There are many wonderful toddler groups and stay-and-play groups run by churches and they do a fantastic job. Most of these naturally have the children as the focus, but I sensed the Lord saying he also wanted to meet the adults in this space. It is a significant season in adults' lives when they are available to come along to church-run daytime toddler groups and are often also open to spiritual refreshment.

Becoming a parent or being a carer of little ones tends to cause us to experience strong emotions. I believe God wants to meet with these adults in this season. Those early years with young children are such a key time in people's lives, especially if they are beginning parenting, and along with the overwhelming feelings of joy and love that they experience for their little ones, there's also the exhaustion, loneliness, isolation and even anger. And I would suggest there is a significant openness to spiritual things, as they explore or re-explore the big questions of life and what they believe. They may be on maternity or paternity leave and returning to work soon, a stay-at-home parent, or be someone who helps provide childcare.

I also really wanted to make a place where they could be introduced to God. The question on my heart for all the young families and particularly the parents/carers was: 'How can I help them meet Jesus?' I wanted the new space to be somewhere the families would be welcomed, encouraged and refreshed; somewhere they might experience something of God's love for them; somewhere the team could draw alongside, befriend, laugh and even cry with them. I wanted to be able to create a space to nurture the whole person – physical, emotional and spiritual – recognising that each of these areas impacts the others and that together they are key to a person feeling whole.

We all need to be nurtured and encouraged, and mums, dads and carers in these crucial first few years need it even more. They are tired, exhausted even, and often overwhelmed by their new role of parenting with all the changes that come with that. I felt that we needed a space where the adults could be nurtured and refreshed to strengthen them and equip them to care for and parent their children and hold their family together. I believe that if we can refresh the parents and carers, we can have a positive impact on how their family will function. If we strengthen the adult, we strengthen the family.

In a stay-and-play group, there is a limited window of opportunity to connect with these adults. I wanted to create a space that would make the most of that and show them something of God's love for them while we had the privilege of hosting them.

A 'Refreshed' model

This started me thinking about how we might connect more deeply and significantly with the adults coming into our church building for the toddler groups week after week and share something of our faith without putting them off. As I prayed about this over a few weeks, a number of Bible verses came into my mind, which I believe were from the Lord. We know that he has a heart for all who are lost and don't know him. The

Bible is a story of how God wants to draw everyone back to himself and bring redemption and restoration. We each have a role to play in this and I began to see that the Lord was calling me to be part of something new in this area.

Various scriptures inspired, encouraged and challenged me as I thought about how we could do things differently to reach all these adults coming into church for midweek playgroups. I hope you will see the journey the Lord brought me on as I considered these scriptures. And perhaps these verses might inspire, encourage and challenge you too.

The first significant verse that impacted my thinking was **2 Kings 7:9**: 'Then they said to each other, "What we're doing is not right. This is a day of good news and we are keeping it to ourselves."' If we had the cure for cancer, we wouldn't invite families into church to be friendly and kind but not tell them about the cure we had. We would want to share that good news with them and show them how to access it. In the same way, we know the power of God in our lives and we recognise that he is the Lord who loves us and has saved us – that is most definitely good news worth sharing, and in fact, we must share it.

The Lord says in **Jeremiah 31:25**: 'I will refresh the weary and satisfy the faint.' My sense was that God wanted to refresh these parents and carers as they came through our doors, so that they might leave in a different state physically, emotionally and most importantly spiritually.

Isaiah 55:1: 'Come, all you who are thirsty, come to the waters; and you who have no money, come, buy and eat! Come, buy wine and milk without money and without cost.' Any community of Christians forming a church has a responsibility and calling to welcome the thirsty. In my experience, parents and caregivers are spiritually thirsty and looking for refreshment.

Then **Isaiah 61:1–3** came to mind:

> The Spirit of the Sovereign Lord is on me, because the Lord has anointed me to preach good news to the poor. He has sent me to bind up the broken-hearted, to proclaim freedom for the captives and release from darkness for the prisoners… to comfort all who mourn… to bestow on them a crown of beauty instead of ashes, the oil of joy instead of mourning, and a garment of praise instead of a spirit of despair. They will be called oaks of righteousness, a planting of the Lord for the display of his splendour.

This is a prophecy from the Old Testament, speaking of Jesus. We are Jesus' hands and feet on this earth, and as we only have one life, let's embrace all God wants to give us to reach out to those who don't know him and live with eternity in mind.

I was mindful that I couldn't do this in my own strength, no matter how well everything was organised or how great the team. It was for God to equip, sustain the vision and bless the outworking of the ministry. I believed this was God's anointing, his calling and his ministry. He was inviting us to play our part in it, which is an honour, a privilege and a great responsibility that none of us would ever want to take lightly.

Psalm 127:1-2: 'Unless the Lord builds the house, the builders labour in vain. Unless the Lord watches over the city, the guards stand watch in vain. In vain you rise early and stay up late, toiling for food to eat – for he grants sleep to those he loves.' I also recognised that it was the Lord's work that he had called me to join in with. For any of us, our labour is in vain if it isn't his ministry with us helping, as opposed to 'my ministry' done in his name. I needed to ensure that I allowed God to be in the driving seat and not in the back seat!

As well as reflecting on these scriptures, I spent a lot of time talking with parents and chatting ideas through with patient friends. I wanted to make sure the new model had the right elements to enable our adult guests to hear about, and hopefully encounter, God. I prayed about it all a great deal, including with good friends who walked with me through all the dreaming and planning. Their input was invaluable, and I couldn't have progressed without them. God provided those friends around me in that season to support and guide me.

Refresh's vision

As a result of the above verses, many conversations and prayers, the vision for Refresh emerged with some distinct, key elements. These are:

Physical refreshment – we would have a simple café area offering tea, coffee, pastries and satsumas, alongside beakers of water and squash and biscuits for the children.

Emotional refreshment – we would have a team of people present to get alongside, encourage and chat to the adults.

Spiritual refreshment – we would give a five-minute gentle Christian thought for the day communicating an aspect of God's love in a relevant and accessible way. We would have a Bible verse each week and would offer to pray for our guests.

— Physical refreshment

We are physical beings with emotions and a spirit. The physical element is obviously important, and I think we understood that even more when during the Covid pandemic we were physically separated from each other. It was so hard not being with those we love, and we weren't able to meet together with friends or have community and belonging, all of which are significant in helping us thrive.

Nourishment and comfort are two key elements to meeting our physical needs, so it was important to create a space where the adults felt physically comfortable. We set up a relaxed café space with adult-sized chairs and tables, hot drinks and pastries. This offered the adults a chance to sit down, even if only for a few minutes, and enjoy a lovely tea or coffee made for them by someone else. When the children are young, their physical needs usually take priority and our own take second place and are often forgotten. To offer the parents something special for them may seem simple but the impact is huge.

— Emotional refreshment

The emotional needs of parents of young ones are significant and varied! They often experience a rollercoaster of emotions and mood swings, with wonderful highs and dark lows. They have the elation of their new child and may experience overwhelming feelings of love for them, but they also have the free-fall lows where their self-esteem takes a dive and they may question who they are.

Parents often feel isolated and lonely, especially as they may be living a long way from any family who could support them. When our children were young, we moved to Tokyo for three years and then to Kuala Lumpur for three years. I have many happy memories of that time, but it was also a time when I felt most isolated and lonely. I was a very long way from family and friends and desperately missed having any support or any sense of community or belonging.

Parenthood brings huge lifestyle changes and there will be an inevitable and significant shift in how parents live and who they see each day.

But it's not just parents who can feel isolated and lonely. Childminders, nannies, au pairs and other caregivers can too. It can be an intense time looking after babies and children, and the adults may really miss having conversations with, and being in the company of, other adults.

— Spiritual refreshment

We are also very much spiritual beings, who are searching for, or at least wanting, meaning and belonging. So offering a short thought for the day might go some way to meeting their spiritual hunger with something wholesome from God. This is the key component that is rarely a part of regular stay-and-play groups or toddler groups, but as churches we can offer this.

I sensed that God wanted to meet these adults at this time, in this particular season of their lives. They might only be bringing children to daytime groups for a few months and then either return to work or the children would move on to nursery or school. So it is important to connect with them and build friendships during this phase. It is possibly our best window of opportunity to introduce them to Jesus.

Resources for thought for the day

When I started to look for material for the thoughts for the day, I struggled to find anything suitable. Everything I came across was often too heavily Christian and aimed at established believers. At the other end of the scale, there is a lot of 'wishy-washy' sayings and self-help, fridge-magnet-style thoughts. There was very little available that I felt would be appropriate for our parents and caregivers/guests. I wanted something definitely biblical yet gentle and accessible to our families who don't yet know God. I wanted to offer some wholesome spiritual food that would feed and challenge our guests. It needed to be particularly relevant to the lives of these adults in the season that they are in.

I searched the internet, YouTube and bookshops, but still didn't find what I felt would be the right thoughts for the day.

As the first term of 13 weeks approached, I was anxious about finding 13 different thoughts! I believed God wanted me to start Refresh, so now I prayed, 'Please, Lord, lead me to the right material. I'm stuck, and I need to prepare for this term. There are 13 weeks, so I need 13 thoughts.' I went to bed worried, and it took me a while to fall asleep. An hour later, I woke up with so many ideas in my head I had to write them down immediately! They came to me in the form of pictures or short phrases which I jotted down in the notebook next to my bed. I said,

'Thank you, Lord!' and went back to sleep. When I woke in the morning, I looked at those outline thoughts written down in the night, and as I counted them, I was amazed to find there were 13! It was exactly the number we needed for the first term. I felt so encouraged and affirmed that this was indeed what God wanted me to do.

This reminded me to rely on God more, so I purposely spent time with him, allowing the Holy Spirit to inspire me and give me the words that would be right for the particular guests we would host: mums, dads, grandparents, nannies and childminders.

I started thinking of verses that I felt would speak to our guests, that we could use at some stage. I collected poems and pictures and put them all in a file so I had a stock of potential material that we could use.

Around this time, a volunteer team member for one of the young families groups I was leading suggested I speak to a lady who had run lots of parenting courses and had also trained as a counsellor and led quiet days with mini thoughts. I contacted this woman and she was so pleased to talk to me. She and her husband were about to move from a large house to a flat and she needed to cull all her files – resources she had collected over the many years for her work. She said the timing couldn't have been better as she had just got everything out to look through and invited me over to help myself to whatever I thought might be useful. It was such a gift! I shared the vision for Refresh, and she really liked the ideas and plans, which was such an encouragement to me personally.

In the next chapters I will unpack what Refresh looks like, how we set up, how each session runs and of course the all-important thought for the day.

2

What Refresh looks like: practicalities and details

With such a bold vision to deliver, excellent organisation of the practicalities and details is essential to ensure the intended experience for our guests is achieved. In this chapter I will describe what Refresh looks like – how we set it up, what we use and why. Each church is different and unique, and I hope this will inspire you to think about how Refresh would look in your setting.

We run Refresh one morning a week for two hours, 10.00 am till noon. We are open term-time only, otherwise we would have many older children joining us and this would radically change the ambiance. Also, some of our team have children at school and they wouldn't be able to help if they had their children with them too.

— Session running order

8.30 am	Setup
9.45 am	Team gathers for chat, snack and prayer
10.00 am	Doors open
11.00 am	Thought for the day
11.30 am	Singing time
12.00 noon	Close and tidy up

Ambiance

The overarching culture of Refresh is prioritising the adults for the morning, and everything is set up with this in mind. The children are made welcome with plenty of toys to keep them engaged. To manage this balance, we set up only quieter toys and children's activities, to encourage calmer play. Refresh is the space where, once a week, the adults are the focus. I think that it is healthy for the children to realise that they are not always the centre of attention and a morning where they take second place is okay, even good for them.

Who is responsible for the children?

The adults maintain responsibility for their children throughout the morning, and the team are there to support them while hosting and facilitating the session. We have found it good practice to put up some signs that say, 'Parents and carers: you are responsible for your children at all times.' This acts as a helpful reminder that we are not looking after their children for the morning, so they do need to supervise them. Any confusion could enable accidents to happen, so it's important from a safety and legal standpoint that everyone is clear.

Setup

The setup is important because it creates the ambiance for the session, so it is worth investing the time in this. The aim is to create a safe and inviting space with clear boundaries and two distinct areas: the café area and the play area.

Setup takes us about an hour and a half as we use a large area, but this might be less for you depending on the size of your space.

We have a couple of team members for the hard setup, namely the furniture (café tables and chairs, sofas, large trestle registration table, chairs in the toy area, children's tables and chairs), a couple of team for the soft setup (mats, toys, signage) and one more team member to set up the kitchen. Please don't feel put off by this. With a smaller space and/or a smaller team, setup can be achieved with less equipment and in less time. The key is to remember the purpose and vision behind Refresh: to create a welcoming space for the adults and a play space for the children. You need to adapt it to your situation. There's no reason why you couldn't do this in one room and split it into different areas, café area and play area, using chairs. Even with ten families in a small room, you can create the Refresh culture.

We place chairs around the room for seating, and these chairs also act as walls to form the boundaries for the play area and café area. We also use chairs to cordon off any unsuitable areas, for example the sound desk and stage, and these we place the wrong way round to form a barrier. This helps everyone to know the areas they are welcome in and the areas that are out of bounds.

There are two diagrams in Appendix 1 that make this clearer: one for setting up in a large space and one for a small venue. The list of preparation to do in advance and on the day can be found in Appendix 2.

We also have a 'Welcome to Refresh Café' sign that we put up outside the church each week.

Café area and kitchen

Our aim is to make the adults feel cared for and valued. We provide refreshments they can enjoy without needing to dig out any money, as it is all included.

The café area is set up close to the kitchen. We have adult-sized tables and chairs, so they are comfortable for our guests. We use attractive tablecloths of PVC 'oilcloth' and an unbreakable vase with an inexpensive artificial flower on each table along with some serviettes. Each table also has copies of the printed verse for the session that guests can take away. All this helps to create the welcoming atmosphere we are aiming for.

The team prepares the drinks and snacks in the kitchen. We offer coffee, a variety of teas, pastries and satsumas, with water and squash and biscuits for the children. You can offer whatever is appropriate in your area and comes within your budget. It's good to aim for it to feel like a small treat for the adults, but even being served a cup of tea and a biscuit is welcoming, kind and always appreciated. We use ceramic mugs for the adults, as we think this creates a more homely feel and is better for the environment than disposable cups, and we serve squash in beakers for the children.

The team serves everything from the kitchen hatch and the children are not allowed into the kitchen. If you don't have a kitchen, you can serve from a large table, as long as you can keep the children away from the hot drinks.

As part of the adult ambiance, we play cheerful, gentle café music in the background. We use a mixture of secular and Christian music.

The Bible verse for the session

A significant element of Refresh is that we have a Bible verse for that week's session. It is on the theme of the thought for that day, and we include this because we believe the word of God is powerful and touches our innermost being. We want our guests to experience this too.

Here's a lovely testimony from a conversation I had with a couple of mums, who used to come to Refresh back in our early days. I will call them Mandy and Jodie. Mandy said she really liked the 'little phrases' we put on the tables each week and that she always took one home and put it on her fridge. Jodie asked, 'What do you do that for?', and Mandy said, 'Because then when I walk past it during the week I read it and it does something to me on the inside!' Jodie replied, 'Really? Well, I'm going to try that, then!' I was able to say that they were verses from the Bible, that they are God's words and that's why they touch us on the inside. Both these women went on to join a daytime group where we looked at the Bible, explored faith and prayed together.

We take the verses from a modern Bible translation, usually the NIV but sometimes from the NLT or *The Message*. Lovely Anne (our oldest team member) prepares the verse. She chooses a relevant picture, including the verse, and then provides printouts which are eight to a page of A4 so they are small enough to cut up. We have these on our café tables for guests to read and take home if they want to, and we read it aloud as part of our thought time. Appendix 5 gives a couple of examples, and a PDF containing full-colour cards for each of the Bible verses used in the thoughts for the day can be found at **brfonline.org.uk/refresh**.

We also have some printed in A5 which we put on the inside of the toilet doors. We find God uses these too, catching people having a quiet moment. One mum told us that she was feeling particularly wobbly one morning when she came into Refresh. She had a sense that God wanted her to have courage, but she didn't think this could really be true. However, when she went to the toilet there on the back of the door was our Refresh verse for the day, Joshua 1:9, which says; 'Be strong and courageous. Do not be afraid; do not be discouraged, for the Lord your God will be with you wherever you go.' That really lifted her spirit and showed her that God was interested in her and knew how she was feeling.

The play area

In the play area we vary the toys a little each week. We lay the toys out on different mats spread out around the room. This makes the space look inviting but also helps the children to settle on to a mat to play with the toys there. We have a list of the toys and equipment needed and a diagram of where to put everything as a prompt for the team. See Appendix 3 for a list of the toys we use and a playdough recipe.

We purposely don't use anything with big wheels or have any ride-ons, as that could encourage racing around. They can enjoy that type of play elsewhere. Our priority is to create a safe play space that encourages engaging and calm play by using quieter toys and activities. The adults really appreciate this!

Baby area

We also have a couple of baby areas, one in the café and one in the play space. We use sofas here as they are particularly comfortable for any breastfeeding mums. We set these up on one side of the café and the play area, rather than in the middle, to create a more sheltered space that feels protected and offers some privacy to the breastfeeding mums or those who would like to sit quietly while their little one is sleeping. We find it works well to place rubber mats on the floor, covered with bright, washable baby blankets, and we provide bouncy chairs and Bumbos. We set out a variety of soft and hard baby toys. It's a mellow and cosy space for those with babies.

We try to keep the toys as clean as possible and once a term we have a team clean-up, which is actually quite a fun time!

Team time

After setting up, we make sure that we have at least 15 minutes of team time before the doors open. This is really important. We gather together around a couple of the café tables, have coffee and a team treat. I try to bake something for us to share, but this isn't essential… although the team sometimes joke that the treat is the only reason they stay on team! Those 15 minutes are vital for a number of reasons. It's time to sit and pray together and to catch up with each other. It's also a time when I can talk about any notices or share information or even go over some safeguarding reminders. Mostly, however, it's a time to connect as a team and take a breath. It gives us a sense of belonging, working together for a common purpose, and it gives us a chance to pray for each other.

We also pray for our morning: that the Lord would indeed meet with our guests. That he would fill us to overflowing with his Holy Spirit so that we might overflow to those who come into Refresh that week. We pray for wisdom and that our words would be encouraging and uplifting. And we pray that every person who comes through our doors would indeed know something more of how much God loves them. We also pray for any specific guests we know who need the touch of God in their lives.

It's a key time to acknowledge and affirm the team. Our team time is a bit like a mini homegroup. I want them to know they are valued and appreciated. Refresh couldn't run without them, so it's important they are cared for.

Welcome and registration

The welcome is so important because we want each of our guests to know that we are pleased to see them and that we want them to have a lovely time with us. We greet each of our guests as they come in and when a person comes for the first time one of the team will show them around and chat to them. This is how we do it.

At 10.00 am we open our doors and have team members ready to receive our guests. We have a team member on the door welcoming and ensuring no children escape! We then have a registration point immediately beyond the entrance and before the café area or play area. We use a large trestle table for this, and you can see the list of what is useful to have there in Appendix 4.

This is where we can again greet each person and write the names of each adult and their children in our register. (See Appendix 4 for a sample register.) We give a name sticker to each adult, with their name in blue if they have been before and in red if they are new. This helps the team identify who is new and they can keep a special lookout for them and introduce them to others.

We charge £3 per family (whether they bring one child or five) and this includes their refreshments for the morning. You need to work out what's appropriate in your area. We have a sign up saying that if a family is on benefits, they don't pay, and most people are happy to tell us if that's the case, or they might let us know during the morning when we're chatting to them in a one-to-one conversation.

We have a petty cash tin and the option to use a contactless card reader.

We don't give name stickers to the children, but we do write their names in the register. We also let them choose a coloured smiley face sticker, which they enjoy doing.

We ask guests to give us a contact number or email address which we enter into our church database for specific Refresh mailouts or emergencies. We put these in a separate Refresh contact list, so our guests don't get the general church mailouts, unless they have requested to receive those.

We request that prams and buggies remain outside, unless of course there is a sleeping baby in it! In that case, the buggy and baby come in, but we ask that the buggy is put outside once the baby is awake. This is because with 65 families most weeks, our whole space would be filled with buggies. Families accept this, as they appreciate how lovely the space is without the buggies. Perhaps in your area the buggies will need to come inside for safety reasons, in which case I suggest you allocate a space to one side where the buggies can be parked so the room isn't cluttered with buggies throughout.

Thought for the day

We have our thought for the day at 11.00 am. I announce this using a microphone because we have a large number of guests, but with a smaller group, a microphone may not be necessary.

After the thought for the day, the morning continues with the café and children playing.

Singing time

At 11.30 am we have our singing time. This lasts for about 15 minutes and the children thoroughly enjoy it. We tidy away a few of the toys and the children and their carers gather with the adults on chairs in an open circle with mats on the floor in the centre for the children. One of our team leads the singing time on her guitar. (We had many years with no guitar, so it isn't essential, but great if you have someone who can play.

Alternatively, you can use songs from Spotify played over a speaker to help you.) They sing a variety of nursery rhymes with actions, and we have some puppets too for songs like 'Old MacDonald had a farm'.

A few years ago, we introduced a Nick and Becky Drake song, 'Big Family of God', which we have as our final song and the children all love it! Everyone, including the adults, joins in. We play the song on Spotify over our sound system, so it is very joyful and uplifting and a perfect way to finish our session.

While the singing is happening, team members set out the toy boxes in the appropriate areas and begin the tidying away. The children help to pick up the toys and put them in the boxes as they get ready to leave.

Finishing and leaving

We finish the session at 12.00 noon. As families leave, we have one of our team on the door to say goodbye and to check that no children leave unaccompanied! We also offer the adults a printed copy of the verse for the day to take home if they would like to. We find this is often a time when some of our guests hang back and we can gently ask if they would like us to pray for them.

Social media

We have created a Facebook page for Refresh which we encourage our guests to follow. We have the QR code with the link to the Facebook page on the screen and on our welcome sign so it is easy for them to access the page. We also have the link on our church website. We tend to post on our Facebook page the day before our session as a reminder and invitation to come and join us. We use this page to communicate the term dates and any special church activities that would be relevant to them.

I hope this chapter has helped you think about how you could run Refresh in your setting. I think the Refresh model can work in a variety of spaces. The main thing is to include the key elements – physical, emotional and spiritual – which can be achieved even in a smaller hall or a couple of rooms. Some questions have been added below to help you think through the practicalities.

- What type of space would you like to use?
- What size is it?
- Could you set up different areas within your space?
- What is the access to the space and how will your guests wait to access the room?
- Where would you be able to store the buggies?
- Does the church have access to a shared card reader or machine?
- Would the church need to source some more appropriate toys?
- Which team members can you think of who could specialise in leading different areas of the morning?

3

Team recruiting, regulations and roles

Refresh is the highlight of my week!
Margaret (volunteer)

Margaret has been on team for seven years. She started volunteering with us while she was still in part-time employment. She is now in her 70s.

The team are crucial not only in being able to just run Refresh, but they also have a significant impact on the 'feel' of each session. They support both the smooth running of the morning and engage in many key conversations. It is a 'client facing' ministry so it's important to consider who you might invite.

> The team make the morning special because they show so much care and they are interested in me which I'm always touched by. It's so nice that the adults get the attention!
> Amy (mum)

There are a number of things to think about in recruiting and maintaining team. It's helpful to work through the following, which I will go into more detail about in this chapter: recruiting; regulations and safeguarding; reasons to join; roles; and retaining team.

Recruiting

— Envisioning and inspiring

It's vital that the team members understand the purpose and vision for Refresh and that they are on board with the ethos. It's important to explain the culture you are trying to establish and your expectations of their role (see 'Roles – flexibility with giftings' below).

Casting the vision and inspiring the congregation with stories and testimonies draws people to want to be part of the ministry. In my experience, when people hear about the vision and that Refresh bears fruit, they want to be part of it. Or if they can't, they are excited about it and suggest others who might be able to join team.

— Gathering and trialling

When someone is interested in being on team, I invite them to come along for a session at Refresh and show them how everything works. If they would then like to join the team, they must complete the paperwork (with the references taken up) and undertake the safeguarding training before they can be on team. This is crucial because we want to ensure we are being as safe as possible. Each team member has a lanyard with their name on, but only once all the paperwork is complete. If we include someone as a member of the team before they have completed all that is necessary, we have not shown due diligence and we are not leading in a responsible way. When we give a team badge/lanyard to a volunteer, we are saying to all our guests (by implication, even if not verbally) that we know this person and they have fulfilled our recruitment requirements.

Our guests trust us, so be very careful to recruit as safely as you can. Taking time to get to know a prospective volunteer is important. If you don't know them very well, perhaps speak to someone else who does.

— Levels of commitment

Levels of commitment from team members will inevitably vary. It is helpful to have a core team who can be present every week, but it also works well to have some team members who commit to coming fortnightly or even monthly. It is important that they communicate this, so we know who is going to be there each week.

Most of our volunteers stay on team for many years, but personal circumstances change and team members may need to step down. I encourage them to let me know as soon as they can, but of course they can leave when they need to.

Regulations and safeguarding

As a church we want to be as safe a place as possible, so safe recruiting is a high priority. In order to comply with this, we use the recommended safeguarding procedure for our volunteer teams, and you will need to follow the procedure recommended by your own church safeguarding team as per Church of England safer recruitment practice guidance or your church denominational equivalent.

Reasons to join

— Different ages and stages

Here are some testimonies from team members:

> It is a pleasure serving on team because it's fun and also because I remember how isolated I felt when I was a mum of little ones. Providing a space where the mums in particular feel cared for is invaluable.
> Jennifer

> I'm there to listen to their stories. As they come to the kitchen hatch for their coffee, they tell me what's going on in their lives. My role is mostly to listen to them and encourage them.
>
> Margaret

Some of our team are parents bringing their children along. Their priority is always their own child, but this is manageable when there are also team on duty without little ones. And having a child with them often helps them to connect easily with other parents. The conversations might be interrupted, as they need to follow their little one, but parents and carers are used to this and can pick up the conversation again.

We have team members who were once guests at Refresh and now their children are at school. These team members have a special heart for Refresh because they remember how much they appreciated the support and encouragement when they were in that season not very long ago.

We have team members who are older and at a completely different stage of life. Some have never been parents and others are now grandparents, but each one has a role to play.

This is Anne's experience. She is in her late 70s:

> There are so many things that I struggle to do as I have a number of health issues including arthritis. I still wanted to use my gifts to bless others but wasn't sure what I could do, so I asked God to show me. Then after chatting with Caroline, I visited Refresh to see if I might have a role. From the moment I went in, I knew that God's idea was a very good one and joined the team in 2017, going every week possible! It was such a wonderful affirmation of how well God knows me (better than I know myself), and it has brought so many blessings.

You can read more of Anne's story in chapter 4.

— Faith levels

Our team is made up of people at various stages in their Christian faith and with different levels of maturity. Some of our team members are new Christians and came to faith through Refresh. They are wonderfully enthusiastic because it was at Refresh they were first introduced to God, and they are keen to share the difference God has made in their lives.

I think being on team has helped all of us grow in faith. Praying for each other and for our guests and seeing answers to those prayers has spurred us on. For those who are new to faith, it has helped model what being a Christian is, and by giving the thought for the day, it has challenged and extended many of the team, despite thinking they would never be able to do that. It's been wonderful to see!

Roles – flexibility with giftings

There are many different possible roles within the team which can be covered by a few people, or if you do have a large team the roles can be shared according to abilities and preferences. These include:

- Setting up and setting down
- Helping in the kitchen with refreshments
- Welcoming and registering guests
- Singing time with the children
- Praying for guests
- Mingling, chatting and connecting new guests with our regular families
- Giving the thought for the day
- Creating the verses
- Making the playdough
- Hosting the 'make do and mend' table

Some of our team like to stick to the same job each week, for example the kitchen team, and others prefer to vary what they do; they might help with registering and welcoming one week, and another week spend more time mingling and chatting. It works best if each team member is able to do the role they enjoy the most, but of course sometimes they need to help out in other spaces too.

The 'make do and mend' table is a wonderful place for more intimate conversations. This is hosted by our oldest team member Anne and draws guests (particularly mums) to go and sit there and chat with Anne while creating something. They often pour out their hearts or have significant conversations. There have been many weeks when Anne has given informal knitting and crocheting lessons too. This is also a table where some of our older children (4+) and those being home educated can learn to sew and make simple felt crafts.

Older team members might not be able to be in the kitchen or move about and mingle safely (too many tripping hazards), but they are such a gift to our guests as they are readily available to chat and probably more importantly to listen. They have rich histories, so can offer the gift of many years of life experience, and their gentleness and wisdom bring a sense of security.

We also need team members to help with setting up and setting down. Some of the team members can arrive early and enjoy setting out all the toys to create an inviting atmosphere; other team members are happy to help set down at the end. I always say to team that they only need to stay as long as they can manage, and they just need to let me know. It's much better that a team member helped for part of the session and then felt keen to return next week than for them to feel exhausted and not want to continue to help. We try to accommodate each team member's individual circumstances as much as possible.

Retaining team – caring for and investing in team

We have an excellent record of keeping volunteers on team. There are a number of reasons for this, most significantly because Refresh is a fun and fruitful ministry to be part of. As we share stories of how individuals have been impacted, it is so encouraging and we celebrate together.

We work as a team with a common purpose, and we support one another. Friendships naturally grow between us and we enjoy working together. It has also been a bridge across generations for older volunteers.

I thank the team regularly and write them each a card and buy a small gift at Christmas, and at Easter I buy all the team a little chocolate egg. Then in the summer we gather for a BBQ to celebrate the year and all that God has done at Refresh. A picnic would work just as well if you don't have somewhere to host a BBQ. The team really appreciate getting together to socialise and having an extended time to catch up with each other. We share stories of Refresh – encouraging ones and some funny ones too.

I try to look out for the individual team members and connect with them between sessions. With a large team this isn't always possible or practical, but a personal text message or email works well too.

We also meet during the year to pray together and listen to God for any words or pictures about Refresh.

It's good to listen to team members and ask them to share any suggestions they have of how we can make Refresh even better. Their input really makes a difference and involving them in how we run Refresh and putting into place their ideas affirm them and contributes to them feeling valued.

So, enjoy gathering and working with your team. In my experience running Refresh not only blesses our guests but also us as a team.

4

Testimonies and stories

This chapter shares testimonies and stories from families who have come along to Refresh, feedback from other churches' experience of running their own Refresh and a story from one of our team.

Louise's story

I moved to Twickenham with my toddler from an area where I had been going to playgroups every day, so I was looking for similar activities in my new area. I found Refresh on Facebook while looking to make friends and asking people what activities they go to with their toddlers. I was specifically looking for a drop-in activity where I could make friends and that wouldn't cost much.

My first experience of Refresh was that so many people talked to me using my name! I think it helps that everyone wears name badges; it takes away any awkwardness. It gave me a feeling of warmth and a sense of belonging. I had often felt invisible as a mum, that it was only the child who was seen. I felt a bit lost as a person and as though my identity was only through my child. I had felt unnoticed in most playgroups, but at Refresh I felt as though I mattered too. That's certainly a significant difference about Refresh. There were always team available wanting to talk and get to know me for who I am myself! The team were friendly, kind and inclusive and that was one of the things that drew me back week after week. It was a drop-in yet an easy place to make friends and get to know the team.

Having the separate café area worked so well and it kept me there longer. I had felt that looking after a toddler and going to playgroups five days a week had become so monotonous, but Refresh felt different. The whole environment is lovely to be in. And having the café area away from the toys made it more of an adult place to be.

I wouldn't have called myself a committed Christian (I had occasionally been to Sunday school, and I attended Brownies and Guides) and as a family only went to church sometimes at Christmas and occasionally at Easter.

The thought for the day was a little seed that got me thinking. Whoever was speaking, it was always someone I could relate to even though I didn't have a faith. When the speaker linked their thought to a Bible verse, that planted a seed and my faith began to grow from there. Some of the Bible verses really touched me and introduced me to the idea that a relationship with God was possible. The thought for the day wasn't a set of instructions on religion, but rather it expressed the nature of faith as having a relationship with God.

I found such a sense of community and belonging at Refresh that I started to bring my children (I have two now) to St Stephen's on Sundays and there I found that same sense of community and belonging. I now have a relationship with God and come to St Stephen's regularly with the children. I feel relaxed coming into church, and I am known.

I've always said I'm not a believer in religion, but now I understand the Christian faith is about having a relationship with God.

Harriet's story

Refresh played a vital role in drawing me and the rest of my family closer to God. I knew the church from living locally, but scarcely ever attended. It was when I became a new mum that I started to come along to Refresh. What I found was a lovely place to come in with my daughter, sit down, chat and play. But as well as the coffee, croissants and colouring, it was a great place to make connections. I started to talk to the Refresh team of volunteers and to other parents and carers there. Friendships blossomed and I wanted to know more about the fellowship of the church community. So I started to come along to the Sunday services and so did my daughter, my mum and my dad. And we have never looked back. We come every Sunday as a family and experience such peace, strength and love as we walk with Jesus and learn to be more like him. The connection I made through Refresh was key in inviting my family into the church community and I continue to cherish the lifelong friends I met there.

Kim's story

I am a full-time worker, a wife and a mum of two children. I'm originally from the Far East and English isn't my first language.

Being a mum of two little boys, I felt isolated, lonely and exhausted. I felt I wasn't recognised as a person but only as a mum with two little boys. I didn't get any family support because they live in another country. My husband seemed always busy with his work or something else. Also, I didn't have friends as some of them left the UK and others didn't have children so they couldn't understand my situation. For example, I couldn't make parties or get-togethers because I couldn't find a babysitter or I couldn't go out as much as before.

My experience of Refresh was a blessing to me. I was emotionally in a very dark place, but their kindness opened my bright side. When I visited them for the first time, they were welcoming to me and my sons. They were so friendly – I thought it wasn't very much like English people, that they wanted to listen to you, support you if they could and pray for you. Also, I liked their little messages on the tables. Those God messages gave me a chance to think about things in my life and life advice.

As a full-time mum with two little children, it was hard to find a place we all could be relaxed. Refresh offered a safe and kind place and warm atmosphere for us. Also, it was the connection point where I came out as a social person, not an isolated lonely mum.

I used to have a negative view of Christians. But Refresh changed my view of them. I guess it depends on who you have met. But I met so many kind, caring Christians through Refresh. They care for people, mums and children and community as God's great message, 'As I have loved you, so you must love one another' (John 13:34).

My Refresh experience is one of the blessings I have in my life. I am always thankful for it.

Claire's story

Four years ago, I was a career woman, with a four-year-old girl and an 18-month-old boy. My career defined me. I had let the cruel world of business grow my insecurities and feed my need for materialism and status. I was a success at business… and on paper it was great. Actually, it was weirdly lonely, exhausting and filled with anxiety.

One day, everything changed. I was on gardening leave; I went from board room to full-time mother. I had no idea what to do with my days or my 18-month-old. Then a school mum recommended Refresh. Oh, gosh: another mind-numbing, chaotic playgroup; what the heck. Remember by this stage my state of anxiety was high, my confidence rock bottom and the situation at home regarding my husband left me with an even bigger problem, so, Refresh it was.

The moment I arrived I felt calm. The organisation was amazing, and kind lovely people asked ME how I was and if I would like a hot coffee and croissant… me! I was introduced to other people with children of a similar age. The time flew by. Towards the end Caroline would talk and contextualise part of the Bible with media that we could relate to, for example a film, a cartoon or an advert. It made sense; I could relate, and left feeling lighter and refreshed – physically, emotionally and spiritually. It got to the stage where I looked forward to Fridays just for Refresh. Talking to Caroline about how I wished they did Refresh more than once a week, she suggested trying church on a Sunday.

Memories came flooding back to me: of tuneless hymns; of preaching to remind me how I was failing as a person, a mother, a daughter and a friend; of a room filled with characters from *The Vicar of Dibley*; and of people I had nothing in common with. Sunday arrived after another stressful and disastrous Saturday at home with my husband, and I craved the safety of Refresh for me and my children. So, off we went to church.

The friendly smell of fresh coffee and croissants greeted me first, followed by many others, including Caroline – all people I could relate to. The children were booked into their age-appropriate group, all organised via iPads, giving ME a break. Jez the vicar stood up, with a mic and iPad and no collar: a regular person. No gown, Bible and lectern separating the holy from us sinners; he was one of us. The God he spoke of was a caring, loving one, not the damning one I had grown up with. I felt safe and happy. Then the worship started with the band playing 'New Wine' by Hillsong. Music that I could connect with, not the hymns that I used to pretend to sing.

All three of us left feeling positive, happy and lighter.

We became regulars, all of us making friends. Then someone mentioned Alpha. An opportunity to ask the questions I was taught not to think, let alone ask, in church. Plus we were fed supper, yes please.

This took everything to another level. I was able to open up about what I had experienced, and how bad I felt. I listened and helped others. Over the eight-week period I watched this amazing group of people change. A widow now at peace and determined to enjoy life; an unhappy husband finding a new job and able to move to the country they had only dreamt of. And me, well, I felt loved and was beginning to accept who I was, not the person I had become due to work and life, but who I was. Family and friends commented on how my sparkle had returned and my prayer of a local job with a company that wanted the real me, which allowed me to properly balance work and life – well, it arrived. My Alpha group and friends from Refresh and church had been praying for my very specific request and it happened.

I now had an amazing relationship with my children, I attended a mother's group, a life group and of course church on a Sunday. I had new friends. A church family accepted and cared for me. When my marriage finally broke down in a very dramatic and ugly way, they were there immediately. My family are hundreds of miles away and before I would have been petrified, but I had my new family who have over the years been there to love and rebuild me and my children.

I am still on a journey with life and God, and I attended a holiday with church which was incredible, experiencing how powerful it is when Christians come together and worship. But what has surprised me the most is how open I now am about being a Christian. Media has stereotyped the church and Christians and it's just not accurate. St Stephen's is a community of loving, generous, non-judgemental humans and it is so relevant to life today. I work in media and I am open and am proud of being a Christian and if that encourages just one person to try Refresh, church or Alpha, then I am delighted and I promise, you will never regret it. I had drifted off the path and was dreadfully unhappy, and God nudged me back on to the right path and has brought the most amazing people into my life, which all started with Refresh.

Adam's experience

I come to Refresh every week with my daughter who is two years old. It's one of the highlights of our week. My daughter loves interacting with other children and she particularly likes eating the croissants! She also loves the singing time.

I really like it as an opportunity to connect with other adults. I look after my daughter during the week, and that time can feel quite solitary. So coming to Refresh and meeting other people has been so good.

The team are super friendly and come and chat and check how I am and how I'm doing, which I really appreciate.

The coffee is good and the snacks are nice too! It's lovely having a croissant and a few biscuits.

Then having the thought for the day gives me a moment to pause and focus. I enjoy listening to the speakers and find that what they share is often quite poignant and aligns with how I am feeling. I find it's just what I need during the week to help me connect with God.

We have also now started coming to church on Sundays as a family, which has been a wonderful chance for us to explore our faith and what God means to us both individually and as a family unit.

Emily's story

What a blessing Refresh was to me, not only when we first were settling in Twickenham, having relocated from Singapore, but also later while I was on the team. I looked forward to a time when not only could my son play to his heart's content, but I was able to connect with friends of all ages both on the team and attending Refresh. It was sometimes the only place I saw those friends, but I am still in contact with many. When the children are small there are few places and activities where you can go, relax and know not only are your children stimulated and happy, but you can leave feeling, well, 'Refreshed'.

When I first started attending, I was quite disconnected and isolated in my faith. Having not regularly attended church or small group for years, having the blessing of attending and later being on the team, I have no doubt the prayers and work the team does was the God-prompt I needed to change. The gentle, encouraging way the team worked meant I didn't feel overwhelmed or a failure at my faith.

There are so many thoughtful elements to Refresh: held within the church; open to all; the short thought for the day; a warm welcoming space on even the coldest, wettest days; quiet spaces, noisy spaces and anything in between. It gives so much at a season in life when not having an adult to talk to for hours on end is a very real prospect.

When looking for a playgroup/preschool a couple of days a week for my son, I made sure our Refresh days were always kept free. I also know I am definitely not the only one who made sure their child-free mornings didn't clash with Refresh.

The encouragement from Caroline and the team meant that once my son was off to school, I was more than happy to volunteer and honoured to have been asked to join the team. If my presence there supported just one person who came even a fraction of the way I was supported while attending with my son, then I am a lucky person.

I was truly blessed to have been able to attend Refresh. The vision for Refresh and how God's work is being done in a non-judgemental, gentle and kind way is truly inspiring.

Since moving away from the UK, Refresh and its team have been in my prayers. I miss them all. It would be a wonderful blessing to any community if Refresh could be replicated in other places.

Kate's story

I came to Refresh very much as a lost sheep. I was new to the area and new to life as a parent! Although I had been brought up in a Christian family, I had wandered off on an atheist route through my career as a neuroscientist. My husband and I had moved out of central London and had children and I had no idea what I was doing or where I was going. I was completely at sea.

I was drawn to Refresh mainly because there was coffee and for the relief of adult conversation! I initially endured the thought for the day, convinced there was nothing in it for me, but the gentle welcome and atmosphere free from judgement softened my heart. It was a slow process but I realised that Jesus was what was missing from my life; he was the anchor I craved; he was the shepherd welcoming back his lost sheep. The leaders at Refresh provided such a loving and gentle space for me to find my own way back to faith. They were always there with a welcoming smile, a listening heart and a shoulder to cry on. Since moving out to the countryside proper, my faith and my children continue to grow and I will be forever grateful to Refresh and St Stephen's for leading me back to the flock, forever anchored in God's love.

Refresh at St Mark's Woodthorpe, Nottingham

For years we ran a midweek toddler church service, with small numbers of families attending, most of whom had some connection to church. We sensed there was more we could offer and had a desire to meet the needs of the parents/carers from the wider community in their demanding roles as primary caregivers, while sharing something of God's love for them. After the pandemic, the need for support was all the greater, with many families yearning for community they had missed over lockdown. As I listened to Caroline present the Refresh model during an online course run by BRF, I realised it was exactly what we needed! A model so simple, yet so effective in sharing the good news.

Our Refresh Community Café has now been running for over a year and the team is stronger than ever. The café is such a lovely place to be and the team enjoy it just as much as the families! We love the simplicity of the approach – fresh pastries, a listening ear, a short thought for the day, a time of singing – and our primary focus always on the adults. We've built strong relationships, prayed for parents/carers and had opportunities to share the good news as we've chatted. There is always an invitation to join us on a Sunday, which several families have accepted. We are so thankful to Caroline for sharing the Refresh vision and are looking forward to seeing God work in the lives of those who come.

Refresh Colchester

In January 2023, we celebrated the tenth anniversary of the Refresh Café at St John's Church Colchester. Inspired by being part of the original team of Refresh at St Stephen's, I gathered some willing volunteers and started a similar café here in Colchester to serve local families with under-threes. Starting a new parents-and-toddlers group meant that we could create the right culture from the very beginning with the values being that the parents/carers of littles ones are able to relax, relate and be refreshed in body, mind and spirit. Serving good-quality refreshments for the adults, with drinks being made to order on arrival and delicious warmed pastries, was seen as a priority. As part of each session, we also offer some 'food for thought' – a member of team shares something on a theme aligned to kingdom values. Many of our guests comment on how different the group is compared to other ones that they attend, and they especially notice the welcome – being greeted by name and treated with love as part of the family.

Refresh meets in the church centre, which was extended in the 1980s, using two linked rooms, typically one set up café-style, with tables and chairs and toddler play activities, and the other room with sofas and soft mats, which is popular with those who bring babies. Each session is a drop-in lasting just under two hours with singing time at the end and birthday celebrations. We usually have 30 families attending during term-time, mostly through invitation by other guests.

For those families who are interested in taking the next steps on their spiritual journey, we have created a pathway for them to access monthly Messy Church and the recently developed Families at 4, which is like Messy Church but more sensory-based play and an accessible Bible story time with puppets. All relevant activities within the church are advertised through our mailing system, which parents and carers are invited to sign up to when they join the group.

The Refresh model has provided a great way of reaching young families and drawing them into relationship with one another and the church. Happy anniversary, St John's! May the next ten years bear much fruit.

Anne's story of how she joined the team

A few years ago, I had a long conversation with God, following a diagnosis of arthritis in my right hip and lower spine. There were so many things that I couldn't do, and I needed wisdom and guidance about the way forward. Having always been involved with various crafts and loved teaching other people and passing on skills, I had confirmation that I should carry on and look for new opportunities to do this.

During a PCC and staff morning in 2017, we were discussing the generation gap in the congregation between our three Sunday services, and

I found myself looking across at Caroline and hearing a God prompt about Refresh. My immediate thought was, 'That's not a good idea, God,' remembering a previous children's group which was very noisy. As the thought wouldn't go away, I asked Caroline whether there was anything that I could do to help at Refresh, such as teaching people to knit or how to sew on a button (as apparently a lot of clothes are thrown away because of lost buttons!). She thought that was a good idea, and having listened to my misgivings, suggested that I visit one morning to see what they were doing and perhaps go in once a month.

From the moment I went in, I knew that God's idea was a very good one and joined the team going every week possible! It was such a wonderful affirmation of how well God knows me (better than I know myself), and it has brought so many blessings.

Someone I knew said that she was surprised when she'd heard that I was helping at Refresh. Having explained how great it was and exactly what went on, I confessed that I sometimes felt a bit guilty – often there's an emphasis on moving 'out of our comfort zone', and God has put me right back in mine. It was such an encouragement when she replied, 'Yes, but he often puts us where we can be the most effective!'

I have to smile sometimes at God's sense of humour – I had such fun recently when a little girl wanted me to go to the playdough table with her. Not being able to use one of the small chairs, I took a big chair over, and spent about an hour pressing out shapes and modelling some animals for them to guess what they were!

Thoughts for the day

5

The thought for the day: what it is and how to do it

> The thoughts for the day always offer hope and inspiration.
> Courtney (grandma)

> I love the thought for the day because I don't get that anywhere else. I don't come to church. It is always varied, not Bible-bashing religion but subtle and relevant for everyone.
> Sophie (mum and childminder)

> The thought for the day gives me something to think about. It's always gentle but gives me that moment to hear something spiritual which is relevant to me.
> Amy (mum)

What is it?

The thought for the day is a very short (less than five minutes), bite-sized, biblical 'taster' that communicates something of God's love for our guests in a relevant way. The aim is to give them a glimpse of who God is, and that he loves them even if they don't know him. It's important to use material that is accessible, without Christian jargon and at an appropriate level without being patronising. Our hope is that a short and purposeful thought for the day will introduce our guests to Jesus and help them connect with him.

This is the hardest part to prepare, so I have included 33 thoughts for the day for you to use in your setting. You can find these in the rest of this part of the book. There are enough to take you through a year of running Refresh. You can use them as they are, or you can adapt them according to your setting. You are welcome to use our stories or swap them for your own examples and stories.

The thought for the day always has a Bible verse that we print off and have on the tables in the café area for our guests to pick up and take home if they wish to. See chapter 2 for more details and Appendix 5 for some sample verses with pictures.

We vary the thought for the day using different speakers. Sometimes one of the team shares a story from their own lives or a story that has inspired them, or I might interview a person (for example, about the marriage course). I may show a clip from a DVD or YouTube and then speak from that.

As time has gone on, I find myself naturally tuning in to things that I think might work well at Refresh. When I am watching a film, I take note of any clip that I could use as part of a thought for the day. I also look at YouTube and type relevant key words + 'Disney/Pixar' into the search bar and watch a lot of clips!

We didn't use video clips for the first few years of Refresh, but if you have the space and the equipment it is an effective tool to draw everyone in and capture the attention of the adults and the children. The children stop what they are doing, sit down and watch (obviously the clip then needs to be suitable for under-fives to see and enjoy). It works well when we find a clip that even tentatively ties in with the thought for the day, as both the adults and the children have paused their conversations and are engaged with the 'thought time'.

I also think about who I might be able to interview. This might be one of the team or a member of our church staff or congregation. Some key questions I focus on are: what difference has God made in your life? Can you tell us about a time God answered a prayer? Tell us about a coincidence that perhaps was a God-incidence?

If a team member shares something difficult that has happened in their life and how they sensed God with them, the harder or sadder the story, the more the guests are tuned in! We don't purposefully look for sad stories to engage them, but we don't avoid them. We acknowledge the troubles of life as well as the joys and we try to strike a balance.

And a warning here; it's important to be sensitive to where the guests might be struggling. If there are difficult topics raised, these must be done sensitively and support offered afterwards. For example, we had one of our team share what happened when their long-awaited baby was born early and very sadly wasn't strong enough to live. Understandably, everyone was in tears! For those who were pregnant in the room, this could have induced huge anxiety, so I gave a caveat before the interview and said that those people might prefer not to hear this thought. I suggested they sit with Anne in the café area (which is linked but a separate space from the main church hall) for the next few minutes. But in what would have been a tragedy for anybody, the speaker was able to share how her faith in God helped in a dark situation.

Another time, we interviewed a woman who worked for Restored – a charity that supports victims of domestic abuse. We had fliers for guests to take away with contact numbers and we also put these on the back of the toilet doors. This thought for the day illustrated God's loving care for the woman who was interviewed as well as providing practical help for any who needed it.

Guests have often approached me many weeks after I have shared something from my life experience in the thought for the day, wanting to know what happened next and how that situation is now.

When to do the thought for the day and how to frame it

Our Refresh morning runs from 10.00 am to 12.00 noon and we do the thought for the day at 11.00 am. As the thought for the day is usually very short, it's important to be consistent and keep to the start time. We have had guests who come just for the thought! I use a microphone now as we have a large space and a lot of people, but if you have a smaller space and fewer than 20 people, a microphone isn't necessary. If your facility has a hearing loop available (as ours does), using a microphone will enable anyone relying on hearing aids to hear easily.

I address everyone together and introduce myself for the benefit of those who are new, and I explain that the aim of Refresh is to refresh you physically (with the lovely tea, coffee and pastries), emotionally (with people to connect with) and spiritually (with the thought for the day, which is something to feed your soul). Then, in order to frame what we are about to do and what our expectation is of them, I ask that they find somewhere to sit with their little ones, pause their conversations and enjoy this time. We then have a two-minute countdown, with music, that plays on the screen and the children enjoy watching the numbers go down and the music reminds them it is time for the thought for the day. Next, I introduce the speaker and the clip (if we have one) and everyone watches. Then I give the thought for the day, connecting it to the clip or explaining why we chose that particular clip.

If another person is doing the thought for the day, they are usually close to me during the two-minute countdown, ready to speak, and I usually say a small prayer of blessing over them during this time. Team members have fed back that this is reassuring and calming.

The verse for the day goes on the screen while the thought for the day is given. We always read the verse aloud for everyone as part of the thought for the day. See Appendix 5 for examples of verses.

To finish our thought for the day, we always offer to pray for anyone who would like that, whatever their situation. I tend to say something like this: 'We believe God does answer prayer and he always hears us, so if you have anything you would like us to pray with you about, or for you or your family, please do come and ask one of us on the team and we would love to pray for you. You don't need to give us any details if you don't want to – we can pray a blessing over your family. If you don't really feel comfortable talking to us, then we also have a basket (with a lid) on our registration table with a notebook and pen, and you can write a prayer request and put it in the basket and as a team we will pray for you after the session.'

Every week we have guests asking us to pray for them, which is such a privilege and God is so good: he answers!

We also give any notices at this point after the thought for the day, or if that would interrupt the moment, we do these before the countdown and the video clip. We include any notices to do with church life that could be relevant to our guests and that they might like to connect with. For example, invitations to the marriage course, Alpha, Christmas services, Me and My Dad (this takes place twice a term on a Saturday morning for dads and their under-fives to connect with other local dads, enjoy refreshments, toys, a bouncy castle and an interactive Bible story).

While I'm talking about notices, I'm pretty strict about not advertising anything else! We have requests for promoting a variety of events from the guests, but I want to keep the focus on Refresh and church. Having this policy makes it easier to say no to everyone rather than having lots of distracting adverts or trying to discern which ones to agree to and which to turn down.

Following on from the thought for the day, we have found it very easy and natural for team members to ask guests, 'What do you think about what Caroline said? Can you relate to that at all?' Because the thought for the day is part of our culture and is the focus point each week, it has been accepted by everyone and they tell me that they look forward to that every time. We regularly have spiritual conversations with our guests, and it is easy for team members to share experiences and stories from their own lives too.

6

33 thoughts for the day for you to use

Here you will find one thought for the day for every session for the academic year. I have put these in categories to help you choose what is suitable for your group each week, but actually many of the thoughts could come under more than one category.

Note: There are some personal stories in the thoughts that follow. You are welcome to use these as they are, change the perspective (e.g. use 'my friend' instead of 'I') or swap in your own stories. I hope they are useful as a springboard for your own thoughts.

Beginning of term

New season 59

Priorities

Jar and stones demonstration 61

Encouragement

Happiness or joy 63
Planted by water..65
God whispers 67

Second chance 69
Belonging – church as family..70
God knows where we are 72

Different seasons and stages of life

Making the best of life's detours..73
Times and seasons 75
Being present...76

God loves us

You say...78
There is more 80
Be who you are 81
Head knowledge to heart knowledge 83
Maya Angelou..85
Being known 87
The Father's love 88

God helps us

God is a very present help 89
Fear..91
Eagle's wings 93

We can make a difference

The cracked pot...95
The starfish story 96

Are you building bridges or walls? 97
Words spoken can't be unsaid 98
Love your enemies 99
I am an influencer 101

Hope

The significance of a name (God's and ours) 103
Precious pearl 105

Special occasions

Christmas preparations 107
Mothering Sunday 109
Easter – sacrificial love 111

End of the summer term

Look after yourself first 112

Beginning of term

New season

> **Do not be anxious about anything, but in every situation, by prayer and petition, with thanksgiving, present your requests to God. And the peace of God, which transcends all understanding, will guard your hearts and your minds in Christ Jesus.**
>
> PHILIPPIANS 4:6–7

▶ **Watch:** *Finding Nemo* clip where Nemo is excited to start school (**youtu.be/eWXOurnVTYg**)

The clip shows Nemo and his dad waking up on the morning of Nemo's first day of starting school. We see that Nemo is very excited, but his dad is nervous. I think we can probably all relate to that!

New things can be exciting, but they can also make us feel nervous or even fearful. How do we hold those two things in the right balance? Stepping into something new – whether it's your child's first day at school, a new job or a new relationship – brings a mixture of emotions.

Our verse today says, 'Do not be anxious about anything, but in every situation, by prayer and petition, with thanksgiving, present your requests to God. And the peace of God, which transcends all understanding, will guard your hearts and your minds in Christ Jesus.'

I'm not sure I can avoid feeling anxious, so when I do, I find it helpful to bring it all to God by just talking to him. I also try to think of things I can thank God for, because that changes my focus and reminds me of

---

Photocopying permitted under CLA Church Licence. Reproduced by permission from Bible Reading Fellowship.

all the good things in my life. And in my experience God does give me peace. It is not a carefree feeling, but rather it is a choice I need to make to trust that God loves me, which he does, and allow his peace to enter my heart and my mind. It's a spiritual exchange, if you like.

(Give your own example of when you have felt anxious and God has given you peace, or use/adapt the following:)

An example: being asked to speak at a women's retreat, I was honoured to be asked but then quite anxious about stepping into something new. I had never done this before. I thanked God for all he had done for me. I recalled the numerous times I had spoken at smaller gatherings to just a few women and sensed that those times were in preparation of this bigger event.

Then I asked him to give me peace and help me prepare for it. Whenever I felt anxious after that, I consciously chose to talk to God about it and ask for his peace. It is a peace that's beyond what I could grasp naturally, and I believe it is from God.

If there are things or situations that you are feeling anxious about at the moment, we would love to pray for you.

Priorities

Jar and stones demonstration

> Trust only in God every moment! Tell him all your troubles and pour out your heart-longings to him. Believe me when I tell you – he will help you!
>
> PSALM 62:8 (TPT)

For this you will need:
- A large glass jar or a medium-sized vase. I use a cube-shaped vase (16cm x 16cm x 16cm) with thick glass so the stones don't cause any damage.
- Four large rocks
- Six big pebbles
- A few cups of sand
- A table to do the demonstration on so everyone can see

Put the four large rocks into your jar/vase. Is it full?

Add the pebbles. Is it full?

Add the sand. Is it full?

The jar represents your life. The large rocks are the most important things – your faith, family, health and friends. The pebbles are the other things that matter like your job, your home and hobbies. The sand is everything else – the small stuff that will fill whatever space it is given.

Photocopying permitted under CLA Church Licence. Reproduced by permission from Bible Reading Fellowship.

If I had put the sand into the jar first, then there would be no room for the pebbles or the rocks. The same goes for our lives. If we spend all our time and energy on the small stuff, we will never have room for the things that are important to us. Take care of the rocks first – the things that really matter – and then the rest will fit in around those.

Take a moment to think about the important things in your life, your priorities. Then think about the things that use up your time and energy each day. Can you adjust your day to prioritise the important things?

It is hard as parents and carers, because there is always so much that needs to be done. Our verse for today reminds us that we can talk to God. We can tell him all our troubles and he will help us.

Encouragement

Happiness or joy

The joy that the Lord gives you will make you strong.
NEHEMIAH 8:10 (GNT)

▶ **Watch:** *Ice Age 4* clip where opossums Crash and Eddie explain 'the secret to happiness' (**youtu.be/sdLw8tSUT_Q**)

I rather like that clip! *Ice Age* is one of my favourite films.

In everyday life, happiness and trials happen concurrently. There are always good things happening for us, but there are also some very hard things to deal with every day – whether personal difficulties, or with wider friends and family, or global issues. There is so much that brings us happiness – our children, families, friends, a sunny day, a favourite meal. But then there are always the really tough things happening at the same time too.

We all have different situations that we find difficult and hard to cope with. Perhaps you are struggling with something at the moment.

(You could give an example here of something you are struggling with.)

How do we cope when so much around us feels so hard?

I wanted to share this verse from the Bible with you. It says that there is a joy that God gives us that makes us strong. And that actually has been my experience. When life is hard and I have asked God to help me, I have sensed his joy – and it is different to happiness. Happiness

---

Photocopying permitted under CLA Church Licence. Reproduced by permission from Bible Reading Fellowship.

is dependent on good things happening to us. It is fleeting, whereas the joy that God gives us is long-lasting and doesn't depend on the circumstances. Our circumstances change and difficult times will come, but we know that God never changes, and when we ask him, he can give us his joy that will sustain us.

If you would like us to pray with you about anything at all, please do ask any of the team.

Planted by water

But blessed is the one who trusts in the Lord, whose confidence is in him. They will be like a tree planted by the water that sends out its roots by the stream. It does not fear when heat comes; its leaves are always green. It has no worries in a year of drought and never fails to bear fruit.

JEREMIAH 17:7–8

(Show a picture of a large green tree on dry land.)

Here is a picture of a large, green tree that is flourishing in the middle of very dry land. It made me wonder how the tree appears to thrive when even survival looks questionable.

The tree flourishes because of its deep roots. The vast root system enables it to draw water and nutrients from deep in the earth, sustaining the tree despite the dry and barren land it is in.

If there's no deep root, everything withers and dries. But if you are sustained by deep roots and have access to water, no matter how hot the sun, the plants stay green because they have an unseen source of water supply that sustains them and enables them to bear the heat.

What is the water that sustains you? Is it something that never runs dry? Does it enable you to bear through in times of heat? And bear fruit?

I remember when my children were young, and I was concerned about keeping the house neat and tidy. I wanted a beautiful environment for them. But with small children it was a constant effort, and I was often getting grumpy and cross. Sometimes we do things with good intentions but don't realise the consequences.

Photocopying permitted under CLA Church Licence. Reproduced by permission from Bible Reading Fellowship.

And one day the Holy Spirit said to me, 'In days to come, your kids are not going to remember if the house was clean or messy. But they will remember if you are cross all the time. Is that the memory you want them to have?'

My way and my good intentions were going to end up with scorched and dry lands, but the Lord brought water. Though the house does not look the way I'd prefer, the trees are green and flourishing. Are the things you are concerned with bringing water and life and bearing good fruit in the long run?

God whispers

> **[God says,] 'Call to me and I will answer you and tell you great and unsearchable things you do not know.'**
> JEREMIAH 33:3

A friend of mine told me recently that she keeps a notebook that she calls 'God whispers'. In it, she jots down moments and occasions when she has wondered if that might be God speaking to her. Perhaps it was in the form of a nudge in her spirit, an impossibly perfectly timed word from a friend or an amazingly encouraging coincidence. Might these have been God?

I really like the way she calls them 'God whispers'. How many times might I have missed something God was trying to tell me because of the distractions and busyness around me? It got me thinking about how I might tune my ear, or indeed my spirit and heart, to listen for God whispers.

In the same way that we can tune in to the particular sounds our individual children make, even here where there are many other children's voices, I wonder if we can tune in to hear God? Perhaps the first step is to acknowledge that God does want to speak to us. Then, as we look out for those moments, we might spot them more readily.

We mostly won't hear an audible voice, but we can learn to recognise his whispers through pictures we might see in our mind's eye, or a sense of love or joy or peace that we feel despite our circumstances. Or it might be something practical like a nudge to phone a friend and when we do, we find that they really needed to hear from us at that moment.

The Bible tells us that God is always wanting to connect with us because he's interested in us and loves us. I think it takes a little practice.

Photocopying permitted under CLA Church Licence. Reproduced by permission from Bible Reading Fellowship.

(Describe a time when you sensed God speaking to you.)

I wonder if you might like to give it a try now. Take a moment and ask, 'God, what is it you love about me?' When I asked God that, I had a feeling inside that God loved my friendliness.

I would love to encourage you to listen for God whispers in your everyday.

Second chance

Forget the former things; do not dwell on the past. See, I am doing a new thing! Now it springs up; do you not perceive it? I am making a way in the wilderness and streams in the wasteland.

ISAIAH 43:18–19

▶ **Watch:** *About Time* trailer (**youtu.be/T7A810duHvw**) – if possible, you may want to cut the bedroom scene

What an amazing gift Tim had. I would love to be able to travel back in time and redo the days I have messed up and change how I responded in those moments. Unfortunately, that isn't possible, so what can we do about all our mistakes and regrets?

As Christians, we believe that through Jesus we can have a second chance. He offers us forgiveness when we get it wrong and hope for the future. He can restore relationships and situations where we might feel they are unresolvable or irredeemable. He waits for us to ask him to help us. If you'd like to know more, please come and ask us! And as always, we would love to pray for you.

Photocopying permitted under CLA Church Licence. Reproduced by permission from Bible Reading Fellowship.

Belonging – church as family

The human body has many parts, but the many parts make up one whole body. So it is with the body of Christ.
1 CORINTHIANS 12:12 (NLT)

▶ **Watch:** 'The Power of Teamwork' video (**youtu.be/4duPBWzf46E**)

We might think that church means the building, and of course to some extent it does. We are in the church 'building' now. But when the Bible talks about the church, it's actually talking about the people. Church is a group of people of all ages and stages meeting together to worship God and journey with each other through life.

We are social beings and thrive in community where we have people around us who know us, encourage us and even challenge us out of love.

We all have different gifts and talents and as we come together, we can help and support each other. We might be strong where another is weak and the same can be true the other way round. The Bible talks about the church family being like a physical body with many parts: hands, feet, eyes, ears – each having a particular role to play, just as we can when we come together.

I don't believe we were made to live isolated and separated lives. Of course we need our privacy and personal space, but I think it's when we have good friends, community and church family around us that we flourish.

Photocopying permitted under CLA Church Licence. Reproduced by permission from Bible Reading Fellowship.

Belonging in our church context gives us a family, whether we have a physical family near us or not. We can act as brothers and sisters to each other, accepting, loving, encouraging and challenging one another as we journey through life with all its joys and trials.

We hope you have a sense of belonging here at Refresh and we invite you to come and be part of our church family. We welcome you whatever your circumstances.

God knows where we are

The Lord is near to all who call on him.
PSALM 145:18

(Show a picture or bring your dog on a lead with another adult. Adapt with details of your own dog if you like.)

This is my dog. She's called Jess. She's a very big black dog and she loves people and children. She also loves to go on a long walk every morning. I'm going to tell you a story about what happened one day when she was on her walk.

We were in the woods and Jess saw a squirrel. She chased after that squirrel, and she ran and ran and went deeper into the woods and then she couldn't find her way back to me. Oh no – she was lost! I was calling her and walking all around the woods, looking for her. I never stopped looking until finally there she was, standing alone, looking sad and lost until she saw me. Then she ran to me wagging her tail. She was SO happy!

Jesus never forgets who we are. He knows our names. He knows who we are and he loves us so much – more than we can ever imagine. So when we feel lost and alone, all we have to do is say, 'I'm here Jesus. Help me,' and he will be right there. He knows what we need even before we ask him for help. Even though we can't see him, he is very real, and he has promised to never leave us. And just like when I was looking for Jess and felt so happy when I found her, so Jesus is so happy when he hears us call out to him. He will always be there for us.

If anyone would like to come and say hello to Jess, line up over in the corner and everyone can take turns stroking her.

Photocopying permitted under CLA Church Licence. Reproduced by permission from Bible Reading Fellowship.

Different seasons and stages of life

Making the best of life's detours

> **The Lord will guide you continually, giving you water when you are dry and restoring your strength. You will be like a well-watered garden, like an ever-flowing spring.**
>
> ISAIAH 58:11 (NLT)

▶ **Watch:** *Cars* trailer (youtu.be/SbXIj2T-_uk)

The *Cars* film is about making the best of life's detours, finding beauty in the journey. I wonder if your life journey is a bit like that. It might not be as you thought it would be, or as you planned.

The life you live now with children may be quite different to the life you once led. Your identity might not be the same as it was in your previous role. New people you meet don't know who you were – like Lightning McQueen, the racing car in the clip.

And whether you are a parent or a carer, life can take unexpected detours. Thinking back to the Covid-19 pandemic and the lockdown we all endured, our lives took a very different turn and were not what any of us imagined life would be like.

How do we cope with life's detours?

Photocopying permitted under CLA Church Licence. Reproduced by permission from Bible Reading Fellowship.

Lightning McQueen, the red racing car, missed his old life and did not want to adapt to where he found himself, but as time went on, he settled into it and then actually began to enjoy it. How can we 'settle in', as it were, to our parent or childcare role without wishing we were somewhere else?

There's a verse in the Bible that I find very helpful, and I believe it to be true. *(Read verse out.)* I have definitely experienced the Lord guiding me and restoring my strength.

Wherever you are on your journey, if you would like us to pray for you about anything, please do come and talk to any of us on the team. We would love to pray God's blessing on you and your situation.

Times and seasons

There is a time for everything, and a season for every activity under the heavens.

ECCLESIASTES 3:1

(Use your own example of a time of illness and needing to pause, or use/ adapt the following:)

A few years ago, I went through quite a long season where I was not well. I'd had tinnitus and vertigo and was just quite fatigued. But I was used to doing a lot of things and suddenly I was struggling to do even very ordinary things like take my kids to school. I just had to do a lot of lying down. And I felt quite frustrated and low.

Then one day God showed me something that really helped me. He showed me that I was in a winter season.

When it's winter, you don't expect the plants to be in full bloom. It's a quiet season and it's about rest, storing up energy for the next season. If the flowers come out too soon and are in the cold, they are not able to withstand it and it takes even longer for the plant to recuperate so that it's in a good place to flower the next season.

What season are you in? In life, we can be in many different seasons at the same time, e.g. in work, health, relationship, friendships, education, family, hobbies. Why is it important to recognise what season we are in? Because it can help us to have realistic expectations in that area and also to put our energies to the right use.

I pray for the eyes of your heart to be opened so that you may be able to clearly see the season you are in and thus make the right choices for the season.

Photocopying permitted under CLA Church Licence. Reproduced by permission from Bible Reading Fellowship.

Being present

[God says,] 'I will refresh the weary and satisfy the faint.'
JEREMIAH 31:25

▶ **Watch:** *The Lion King* – 'I just can't wait to be king' **(youtu.be/0bGjlvukgHU**, from 1:33 to 3:30)

How often do we wish we were in a different season, or we want to rush ahead and skip where we are now? Perhaps we look at those around us and wish we had their life.

I would love to have grandchildren. I feel I am a grandma-in-waiting. My grown-up children, though, are busy with their lives, and it doesn't look as though my dream will be fulfilled anytime soon. So, what do we do?

I think I have a choice: I could waste my time wishing I had grandchildren and hoping for the day that particular dream might be fulfilled, or I can make myself present in the here and now and invest in those right in front of me.

I am blessed with knowing a young family and even more blessed that they have become close friends. I have the privilege of being in these children's lives. They are my 'borrowed' grandchildren, as it were, and I love them deeply. I believe God has given me this family to support and encourage through this season where I can be a blessing to them, and they are most definitely a blessing to me!

Where are you at the moment? Is it where you want to be? How can we learn to be content where we are and learn all we need to in preparation for the next season?

Photocopying permitted under CLA Church Licence. Reproduced by permission from Bible Reading Fellowship.

Sometimes in this season of bringing up children, whether as a parent, grandparent or carer, we can feel as though we just want to get to the next season. I just can't wait for… the crying to stop, my little one to sleep through the night or to have more than five minutes of my own uninterrupted thoughts! But let's not wish away this time. It will go quicker than you think and one day you will be in a different season. God is always ready to refresh us when we are feeling weary. He won't ever force himself into your life, but he waits for you to ask him to refresh you.

Can I encourage you to give it a try, if you are feeling weary today? Some things we just can't do in our own strength and actually we don't need to!

Enjoy being refreshed here – and take us up on our offer to pray for you.

God loves us

You say

> For you created my inmost being; you knit me together in my mother's womb. I praise you because I am fearfully and wonderfully made; your works are wonderful, I know that full well.
>
> PSALM 139:13–14

▶ **Watch:** Lauren Daigle song 'You say' (**youtu.be/slaT8Jl2zpl**)

This is such a beautiful song, sung by Lauren Daigle, which she also cowrote with her producers. The song begins with the voices we hear in our minds that tell us that we're not enough and that we'll never measure up!

I can certainly relate to that. So often we have negative thoughts, and they can be quite crippling. We can get stuck in negative thought patterns that go round in our minds.

There's an old saying that says, 'You can't stop birds landing on your head, but you can stop them nesting in your hair!' Negative thoughts will arrive in our minds, but we need to be quick to throw them out and replace them with truths. I agree with Lauren Daigle's words as the song continues. We need a reminder of who we are in God's eyes.

When life is hard (and it so often is!) I have found a couple of techniques that really help me get back to the right frame of mind and perspective.

Photocopying permitted under CLA Church Licence. Reproduced by permission from Bible Reading Fellowship.

First, I remind myself who God is, his character, and I focus on these:

- He is almighty God. He is loving and kind.
- He is my heavenly Father, my redeemer, my shepherd, my saviour.
- He is my refuge, my fortress, my rock and my anchor.
- He is my hope.

Then I remind myself who I am in God and how he sees me:

- I am his child, and I am redeemed.
- I am fearfully and wonderfully made.
- I am a blessing.
- I am hidden under his wing, and he loves me just as I am.

Which do you need to be reminded of today?

Photocopying permitted under CLA Church Licence. Reproduced by permission from Bible Reading Fellowship.

There is more

No eye has seen, no ear has heard, and no mind has imagined what God has prepared for those who love him.
1 CORINTHIANS 2:9 (NLT)

Have you ever wondered what it is like to get to know Jesus and live a life with him?

It's full of unexpected wonder, beauty and surprises.

(Show two pictures: the first one of a snowflake magnified many times and the second one of the night sky as seen through a telescope, for example Constellation Andromeda.)

I wonder if you have every looked at anything under a microscope. This is a snowflake magnified many times. What strikes me is that when we look at the snowflake with the naked eye, we see only the basic structure. But when we see a magnified version, there is so much more.

In the same way, when we look up at the sky at night and see the stars, we see only a tiny portion of what is actually there. If we look through a telescope, it radically enhances our view, and we see so much more.

As Christians, we believe God has so much more that he wants to show us. God is in the vastness of the universe and in the tiny details of the smallest atom. He sees the big picture and he knows the details of our lives.

And there is more.

God loves us and has so much he wants to share with us. And he is inviting you on this journey to discover more.

Photocopying permitted under CLA Church Licence. Reproduced by permission from Bible Reading Fellowship.

Be who you are

I thank you, God, for making me so mysteriously complex! Everything you do is marvellously breathtaking. It simply amazes me to think about it! How thoroughly you know me, Lord!

PSALM 139:14 (TPT)

▶ **Watch:** *The Secret Life of Pets 2* trailer (**youtu.be/mYocfuqu2A8**)

I really like that clip, as it reminds me how we can spend much of our time trying to be like someone else. I read recently that the number one regret of the dying is: 'I wish I'd had the courage to live a life true to myself, not the life others expected of me.'

I think it's interesting that we have a fascination with programmes like *Who Do You Think You Are?* and DNA sites. We want to understand more about ourselves and where we've come from. We want to know who we are in the deeper sense.

We all have different gifts and talents, and perhaps if we could have chosen them, we would have picked alternative ones. Sadly we can't choose our talents, but we can choose what we do with those we have.

Michael is an example. As a child he was ridiculed for his big hands and big feet. But when he got into the swimming pool, he found what he was good at. His big hands and feet were an advantage:

> The things that held him back when he tried to be like others, were his greatest strength when he decided to be himself. What made him a source of ridicule on land, made him a world beater in water. His surname is Phelps. He won 18 Olympic gold medals and set many world records and is one of the greatest Olympians ever.
> Rob Parsons, *The Wisdom House*, chapter 3

Photocopying permitted under CLA Church Licence. Reproduced by permission from Bible Reading Fellowship.

In fact, who we become is a combination of our gifts and our life experiences. It might be possible to genetically clone Beethoven, for example, but the result wouldn't be the same because there was more to Beethoven than his genetic make-up, and the same is true for us.

Rather than wishing you were someone else, I would love to encourage you to accept the uniqueness of who you are, embrace it. No one else can be you!

Psalm 139 reminds us that God knows and loves us completely.

Head knowledge to heart knowledge

O Lord, you have examined my heart and know everything about me. You know when I sit down or stand up. You know my thoughts even when I'm far away.

PSALM 139:1–2 (NLT)

Knowledge is like underwear – good to have but not something to show off!

We went on holiday this summer. Before we went, we read quite a bit about the different things to do – the walks, the beaches, the nice places to eat – and we also asked some friends who know the place well to tell us about it. They described different places to go and shared why they liked it. But then when we were actually there, and we experienced it for ourselves, that knowledge somehow moved from being only in our head, or intellectual knowledge, to our hearts, our experiential knowledge. When we experience something, we know and understand it in a fuller, deeper way. There's a 'connection' because of the encounter.

It can be the same with people. We can 'know' about people, and we can 'know' people. What's the difference? I suggest it develops as we spend time with that person. We can know a lot about them, but it is a different kind of knowing when we have a personal connection with them. We become friends and there's a deeper understanding between us.

I think it is also the same with God. We can listen to other people's experiences of God. We may have knowledge of God, but if we spend time in his presence, we can know him personally. I believe that is possible through Jesus.

God is not like a celebrity who we can only know about but can't get access to. The Bible tells us we have access to God the Father through

---

Photocopying permitted under CLA Church Licence. Reproduced by permission from Bible Reading Fellowship.

Jesus. We can come into the presence of God. What a privilege! And what's more, while we are getting to know him, he already knows us completely.

I personally find it so reassuring that even though God knows all about me, he loves me anyway. I know my friends love me, but God's love for me is *more*.

I would encourage you if you don't already know God, to perhaps start to talk to him today. He is ready to hear you.

Please do talk to me or any of the team if you would like to know more.

Maya Angelou

The Lord your God loves you!

DEUTERONOMY 23:5

Maya Angelou died aged 86. She was an internationally celebrated poet, author and civil rights campaigner. In addition to her trove of writings about her heartbreaking childhood, her convictions on civil rights and dozens of film, television and play scripts, Maya Angelou often wrote about her faith as well.

In one interview, Maya said that it was her faith in God that allowed her to achieve such incredible feats. She said:

> I found that I knew not only that there was God but that I was a child of God. When I understood that, when I comprehended that, more than that, when I internalised that, ingested that, I became courageous.

In one of her books, Maya describes how she was asked to read to her voice teacher a section which ended with the words, 'God loves me.' She was asked to repeat numerous times, 'God loves me', 'God loves me', God loves me', and then she writes:

> I thought that there might be a little truth in the statement. There was a possibility that God really did love me, me Maya Angelou. I suddenly began to cry at the gravity and grandeur of it all. I knew that if God loved me, then I could do wonderful things, I could try great things, learn anything, achieve anything. For what could stand against me, since one person, with God, constitutes the majority?
>
> Maya Angelou, *Letters to my Daughter*

Photocopying permitted under CLA Church Licence. Reproduced by permission from Bible Reading Fellowship.

She went on to say:

> It still humbles me that this force which made leaves and fleas and stars and rivers and you, loves me. Me, Maya Angelou. It's amazing. I can do anything. And do it well. Any good thing, I can do it. That's why I am who I am, yes, because God loves me and I'm amazed at it. I'm grateful for it.
>
> Maya Angelou in interview with Oprah (**oprah.com/omagazine/maya-angelou-interviewed-by-oprah-in-2013/2**)

I find it quite striking that such a simple phrase would impact this prestigious writer so greatly. And perhaps that's all we need to know, really – that God loves us! I wonder if you might try repeating that to yourself, just as Maya did, and see if it helps you understand the truth of that more.

Being known

I am fully known.

1 CORINTHIANS 13:12

I regularly walk to our local shops, and one of the things I enjoy most about that is bumping into people I know. We might stop for a chat, or we might just say hello. It gives me a sense of being known. When I go to the supermarket, there's a checkout lady I particularly like. I try to join her queue when I can, because she is always friendly and asks me how I am. It makes me feel known in my community.

(This is my story, but you could either use a personal one of your own, or introduce it as 'my friend's grown-up son'.)

When my grown-up son and daughter-in-law went on holiday to Thailand, they also went over to Kuala Lumpur, as that's where we lived as a family when my son was a child. My son wanted to show his wife where we had lived and some places where we spent much of our time as a family. After going to see our old house, they popped into the mini market round the corner. The Malaysian couple who own it recognised my son immediately, even though it had been 15 years since we had left Kuala Lumpur. He was absolutely blown away by that! They chatted for a while and then he sent me a photo of him with them there. My daughter-in-law also texted me later to say that he hadn't stopped grinning ever since. It struck me how important it is to us to be known.

We need to belong. When we are known by others, we feel secure and loved. It's great to be known by those around us and I hope you have a sense of being 'fully known' here at Refresh, but it reminded me how wonderful it is that we are known by God. He knows us and loves us more than anyone ever will.

Photocopying permitted under CLA Church Licence. Reproduced by permission from Bible Reading Fellowship.

The Father's love

> **See what great love the Father has lavished on us, that we should be called children of God! And that is what we are!**
>
> 1 JOHN 3:1

▶ **Watch:** *Finding Nemo* clip where Nigel tells Nemo about his dad's adventures (**youtu.be/Cwd3A9l0Ib0**)

This is such a great clip. Nemo is in the dentist's fish tank feeling very miserable. He desperately misses his dad and wants to go home.

Along comes Nigel the albatross and tells Nemo that his father Marlin has been searching the oceans for him and fighting sharks along the way. It's lovely to see the impact that news has on Nemo. Despite his circumstances remaining the same – as he remains trapped in the fish tank – that news impacts Nemo hugely and his whole demeanour changes because he realises his father loves him.

This is a helpful picture of how different we can feel when we understand that God loves us. Knowing we are loved by our heavenly Father can make a significant difference to how we cope in difficult circumstances. In my experience, knowing God loves me gives me courage and hope. I can trust him to be there even in the darkest moments. God promises to never leave us.

Do you know God loves you with a perfect Father's love?

Photocopying permitted under CLA Church Licence. Reproduced by permission from Bible Reading Fellowship.

God helps us

God is a very present help

God is our refuge and strength, an ever-present help in trouble.
PSALM 46:1

▶ **Watch:** *Aladdin* – 'Friend like me', from 1:40 to the end (**youtu.be/Qx91ff77yzM**)

Who wouldn't like a friend like the Genie? In the clip, Aladdin was stuck in a cave and the Genie helped him to get out.

This morning, I want to share a story about how God is an all-powerful friend who helps me whenever I need him. I call on him whenever I'm in trouble or in need of help.

(Tell your own similar story, or use/adapt the following:)

When I was younger, living in Australia, I was driving home late at night and a voice in my mind said to me, 'You should get in the left lane, close to the curb, because you're going to get a flat tyre.' That's strange, I thought, because I was young and had never changed a flat tyre before.

Sure enough, a few minutes later I had to pull over as the tyre was flat!

I knew the voice must have been God, so I prayed – what do I do now? Just then, a car pulled up in front of me, and a man got out. He had a woman in the car with him who stayed in the front seat, but he said, 'Would you like some help with your tyre?'

Photocopying permitted under CLA Church Licence. Reproduced by permission from Bible Reading Fellowship.

It turns out the man was an off-duty policeman and saw that I needed some help, so just decided to stop on his way home! I was so thankful and have never forgotten the story about how God helped me by sending me a message and then a helper when I needed him.

God is not like a genie in a bottle, but he promises to never leave us and to help us if we ask. Today's Bible verse helps me to remember that promise.

If you feel like you need God and want to ask him to help you, any of the team here would love to pray with you. Just see us afterwards or write down a prayer to put in the box on the welcome desk.

Fear

The Lord is with me; I will not be afraid.

PSALM 118:6

At one level, fear is healthy. 'Fear' is an emotion induced by a perceived threat. It is a natural human emotion. It is a basic survival mechanism. It keeps us alive. It protects us from danger. It is God-given.

However, there is also such a thing as unhealthy fear. The Greek word commonly used in the New Testament is *phobos* – from which we get the word 'phobia'. This is unhealthy fear. It is disproportionate to the danger posed. A helpful acronym to define fear is 'False Evidence Appearing Real'. It is when we catastrophise – overestimating the danger and underestimating our ability to cope.

Common phobias include fears in relation to health, finances, failure, growing old, death, loneliness, rejection, messing up, public speaking, flying, heights, snakes and spiders. They also include such things as what is now called FOMO – the fear of missing out, the fear of not being special.

In my own life, I have experienced many of these fears – from a fear of failure to a fear of something awful happening to my children and other irrational fears – fears about public speaking and a fear of missing out.

The Bible says there is a healthy kind of fear – the fear of God. This does not mean being frightened of God. In fact, it means the opposite! It is an understanding of who God is in relation to us. It means respect, reverence, awe, honour, adoration and worship; and it could even be translated as love for God. It recognises the power, majesty and holiness of God almighty. It leads to a healthy respect of God and is the antidote to all other fears and phobias we experience in life. Fear God, and you need not fear anything else or anyone else.

Perhaps it is no coincidence that as the fear of God has decreased in our society, all the other fears have increased. We need to return to the right relationship with God.

The expression, 'Do not be afraid,' appears in the Bible 366 times – one for every day of the year (including leap years!).

Eagle's wings

But those who hope in the Lord will renew their strength. They will soar on wings like eagles; they will run and not grow weary, they will walk and not be faint.

ISAIAH 40:31

(You might want to provide origami paper cranes on the café tables, but this is optional.)

I've been feeling particularly tired the last couple of weeks, and I remembered this passage in the Bible that is one of my favourites. I believe God does care for us and will support us through tired times when we ask him. He can restore our souls. It's such a lovely picture of the eagle soaring in the air. I'll read it again and perhaps let's just imagine that for a minute.

I believe God also provides people around us who can help, support and encourage us.

I read recently about migrating geese, which I found fascinating and relatable. The birds are on a mission – they are migrating to warmer climates. They purposely fly in a particular direction in order to reach their destination. It is hard work and very tiring, but they press on to reach that goal.

We too have a purpose; at the moment it's raising or caring for children. It is hard work and very tiring, but we keep going. We may have other purposes too.

Then I read about how the birds fly in 'V' formation and the reason why they fly in in that way. The lead bird 'breaks up' the wall of air that the flock flies into. The swirling air caused by the lead bird's movements then helps to push along the birds behind it. The 'V' formation gives every bird behind the lead bird the same sort of assistance and push.

Because this is hard work for the lead bird, the lead drops back after a short while so another bird takes on the work of the lead. It has been shown that birds in the 'V' formation can fly a full 70% further than a bird flying alone, because of the much easier flying the 'V' formation provides.

That isn't the only reason for the 'V', however. The birds often do not fly close enough to realise the full benefit of that shape. For geese, the 'V' also gives them the ability to watch each other and communicate about likely landing locations. They honk to each other regularly while they fly.

Geese are very loyal birds. A male and female will mate for life. A family group will stay together even within the flock. Often when you watch a 'V' formation, you will see a group of birds that stays as a unit, breaking off together when the flock comes down to land. If a bird in the flock becomes injured during migration and can't keep up with the 'V', a few family members or flock mates will go down with the injured bird to keep it safe while it recuperates. Only when it is ready to fly (or succumbs to its injuries) will they take off again, looking for a new flock to join up with.

There are times when we are in front and times when we are behind and need our fellow birds to honk encouragingly at us to help us keep going. And there are times when we fall out of formation and need a great deal of help and support. And it's in those times too when we can ask God to help us and restore us.

(If you have the origami cranes out.) We have put origami birds on the tables for you to take home if you would like as a reminder of this morning's thought.

Photocopying permitted under CLA Church Licence. Reproduced by permission from Bible Reading Fellowship.

We can make a difference

The cracked pot

> A good person produces good things from the treasury of a good heart... What you say flows from what is in your heart.
>
> LUKE 6:45 (NLT)

Sometimes we feel unhappy with ourselves because we are not perfect. We recognise all our flaws and focus on those. Here's a lovely story that illustrates how beauty can come out of brokenness and how it's often through our brokenness that we give life and joy to others.

(Read 'The Cracked Pot' by Sacinandana Swami from **snswami.wordpress.com/2015/08/17/the-cracked-water-pot***.)*

Despite our imperfections, we can bring joy to those around us. We can offer encouragement and kind words and make a difference just where we are.

Photocopying permitted under CLA Church Licence. Reproduced by permission from Bible Reading Fellowship.

The starfish story

[God says,] 'I will refresh the weary and satisfy the faint.'
JEREMIAH 31:25

(Read 'The Tale of the Starfish', adapted from The Star Thrower *by Loren Eiseley from* **thestarfishchange.org/starfish-tale**.*)*

I think this is a lovely picture of how our small and seemingly useless actions can make a profound difference. Perhaps sitting down and sharing a cup of coffee with a friend doesn't seem much, and it doesn't take a lot of effort for us, but it can mean a huge amount to the other person, and it can make a difference to their day. It's the little things that are important to our children and partners too. Take time and make the most of the 'moments'. Take time to make eye contact, offer a smile or a kind word and see what a difference it makes. It may only be a small thing, but…!

We so want you to feel refreshed here and hope that you do. Take time to enjoy a lovely cup of coffee, talk to a friend or one of our team… make the most of a few 'slower' moments!

Photocopying permitted under CLA Church Licence. Reproduced by permission from Bible Reading Fellowship.

Are you building bridges or walls?

So then let us pursue what makes for peace and for mutual upbuilding.
ROMANS 14:19 (ESV)

(Read 'There Once Was a Carpenter' by Karl Eckhoff from **sermoncentral.com/sermon-illustrations/15682/there-once-was-a-carpenter-who-visited-one-of-two-by-karl-eckhoff**.*)*

May you be a bridge or a builder of bridges.

People are lonely because they build walls instead of bridges.

So then let us pursue what makes for peace and for mutual upbuilding.

Words spoken can't be unsaid

Be gentle with one another, sensitive. Forgive one another as quickly and thoroughly as God in Christ forgave you.
EPHESIANS 4:32 (MSG)

(You will need a flower with lots of petals – a dahlia or chrysanthemum works well.)

Here is a flower which has lots of petals. Each of the petals can be pulled off, one by one. *(As you're talking, do just that, taking off the petals and dropping them on the floor.)* It's very easy and quite a fun thing to do!

Now, is there someone who would like to come up here and help me? We're going to try and put all the petals back on the flower… is this too difficult? But it was so easy to take them off!

This is a little bit like when we say bad things about someone. It can give us a weirdly nice feeling to criticise someone and that's like taking the petals off the flower. The words have been spoken – they can't be unsaid – and it's difficult to make it better. Let's be careful what we say about each other. Let's not say horrible things about someone and let's be kind instead. Remember what happened to the flower!

Love your enemies

> **But I tell you, love your enemies and pray for those who persecute you, that you may be children of your Father in heaven.**
> MATTHEW 5:44–45

▶ **Watch:** 'Love Your Enemy' video (**youtu.be/1saflRVkpDk**, from 0:15 to 2:28)

If I said the word 'conflict' to you, what would your first reaction be? Would you be ready to run into a fight and defend yourself, or would you be more likely to cringe at the word and want to avoid the first sign of discord?

If you're like me, you might want to avoid conflict, and the thought of having to resolve an argument or disagreement is so uncomfortable, you'd just rather leave it alone and then think about it over and over again, taking more of the worry on to yourself than you need to!

I won't ask for a show of hands, but I'm sure we could put ourselves in either camp.

Recently, I seem to be coming up against a bit of conflict – in my relationships at home with my husband or with my children, even conflict with service providers – I just don't seem to be able to find a builder that's affordable and available to fix our garden wall!

And conflict *between* my children seems to be getting worse at the moment. So I've just been wondering, what do I do about this and how can I get better at managing conflict?

Then I remembered this verse from the Bible, that some of you might have heard before.

Photocopying permitted under CLA Church Licence. Reproduced by permission from Bible Reading Fellowship.

In the examples I gave just now of conflict, I wouldn't necessarily call these people my 'enemies', but I believe the principle is the same. When I'm in conflict with someone, this verse *reminds* me to pray for the people that I'm frustrated with or fighting with.

This verse also *promises* me that I will be more like God – and what is God like? I believe as a Christian he is loving, kind, joyful and at peace.

So my encouragement today, if you're in conflict in any of your relationships, is to remember to pray for them, think good thoughts towards them and want the best for them. When you do, you might just find yourself at peace with them and the situation itself.

If you would like prayer for any conflict or help to pray for anyone that you're in conflict with, please let the team know.

Photocopying permitted under CLA Church Licence. Reproduced by permission from Bible Reading Fellowship.

I am an influencer

> **When hard pressed, I cried to the Lord; he brought me into a spacious place.**
> PSALM 118:5

Lots of people nowadays want to be internet influencers – but actually we are all influencers, whether we aim to be or not. Our speech and our actions impact those around us, particularly those close to us, such as our family and more specifically our children.

Have you noticed how your children copy what you say and may repeat something you have said when you least expect it or, more embarrassingly, in front of the people you least want to hear it? We might not have even been aware that we said it, but our children absorb so much more than we realise.

When we are under pressure as a parent or carer, with all the demands of the children and all the tasks we need to complete, we may feel hard pressed on every side. Our patience runs out sooner than we would like it to.

What we're full of is what will spill over when we are knocked. So, if we are full of anger and frustration, that is what will spill over when we are pushed. If we can instead be full of love, joy and peace, then those are the things that will spill over when we are provoked and impact those around us.

We know that what we physically put into our bodies affects how we function and how much energy we have. To keep ourselves healthy emotionally, we need to be loved and encouraged. With young children around, we can neglect our emotional and spiritual health. Perhaps our bodies shout louder when we are physically hungry, so we manage to

---

Photocopying permitted under CLA Church Licence. Reproduced by permission from Bible Reading Fellowship.

keep fed and hydrated. But what about emotionally and spiritually? Those can be much harder to nurture and care for when we're busy with young children.

We know we need good food and plenty of water for our physical health, but what do we need for our emotional and spiritual health?

Something I suggest is to fill your mind with good things. Research has shown that thankfulness and gratitude have a positive impact on our state of mind, and interestingly the Bible encourages us to do this. We can listen to worship music or read the psalms (which are prayers written by a variety of people in all sorts of situations – cries of the heart to God). And we can talk to God ourselves. There's no special formula – we can just chat to him! Drawing on God can help fill up our emotional and spiritual tank with good things that will then spill over to those around you.

I would love to encourage you to 'fill up on God' so you can be refreshed and restored.

Hope

The significance of a name (God's and ours)

> **Truly my soul finds rest in God; my salvation comes from him. Truly he is my rock and my salvation; he is my fortress, I shall never be shaken.**
>
> PSALM 62:1–2

▶ **Watch:** *Paddington* clip where Mr Brown joins Paddington for tea (**youtu.be/VBku6tXLDo4**)

Names are significant. My name was given to me by my parents and it's what I'm known by. We spent a long time choosing names for our children and, although we didn't particularly choose names because of their meaning, we did take that into consideration. When my friend had twins, she named them Isaac and Barnaby, which mean 'laughter' and 'encouragement', because they felt they would need a lot of both of those! But whatever name you choose, it becomes synonymous with your child.

In the Bible God has lots of names, approximately 50, as each of those names highlights a particular character trait and so helps us understand him more. The names of God reveal who he is.

God is called Father, rock, shepherd, everlasting, provider, healer, alpha and omega, almighty, creator and many more. For me, different names of God have been helpful in different circumstances.

Photocopying permitted under CLA Church Licence. Reproduced by permission from Bible Reading Fellowship.

I wonder if you have any difficult things in your life that you are coping with at the moment. Perhaps it's sadness, and you need comfort. Or fear, and you need peace. Whatever you are dealing with, I suggest choosing one particular name of God, whether that's Father, rock, provider or healer, and focus on that for a moment. Then ask God as Father, rock, provider or healer to help you in your situation.

(Give your own example, or use/adapt the following):

I found it overwhelmingly sad when my mother was seriously ill in hospital, and I felt very wobbly. Remembering that God is my rock really helped me feel secure when everything around me felt as though it was crumbling away.

Which name or character of God would be helpful for you to focus on today?

Precious pearl

I pray that God, the source of hope, will fill you completely with joy and peace because you trust in him. Then you will overflow with confident hope through the power of the Holy Spirit.

ROMANS 15:13 (NLT)

Pearls are often given as a precious gift. You might already know that they are formed as the result of an irritant, usually a parasite, entering the oyster. This irritation encourages the oyster to secrete layer after layer of a substance called nacre, which surrounds the parasite. These layers build up, eventually forming the beautiful pearl.

It's not a quick process: pearls take a long time to form, which is what makes them precious. The end result is unrecognisable compared to the original irritating parasite that started the process.

Rather like the pearls, we too are precious and we take time to reach our full potential and fully become who we can be.

I read recently that we actually need adversity and setbacks to reach our fullest level of development and growth. Just as the pearl would not develop without the irritating parasite, adversity causes us to grow in ways an easy life can't.

It has been suggested that there are three attitudes to adversity: hope, despair and resignation. I wonder which resonates with you at the moment.

Another thing that struck me when thinking about the pearl and the oyster was that while the whole process of pearl formation is taking place, the delicate oyster is completely protected by the strong shell. This image reminds me of God's loving hands around me, protecting me despite any irritations I may be struggling with, helping transform the irritations into something beautiful.

We believe God is a God of hope and the Bible verse on the tables describe this. We would love to pray with you about any irritations or stresses in your life. Please do come and ask us.

Special occasions

Christmas preparations

[Jesus] said, 'I am the light of the world. Whoever follows me will never walk in darkness, but will have the light of life.'

JOHN 8:12

Watch: 'That time of year' from *Olaf's Adventures* (**youtu.be/nLGBEETtEPc**)

In the clip, we saw Olaf the snowman exploring the numerous different traditions people have at Christmas. There is quite a range, but interestingly many of the traditions include lights. We put lights on our Christmas trees, around our houses, in our gardens and even many of our streets are decorated with them too. In the Bible, Jesus is called the 'light of the world', so all these Christmas lights can help remind us of Jesus.

Let's think about what light does.

Light helps us see a situation clearly. It reveals the truth.

Light is reassuring. If I am worried about something, it feels much worse in the night and it is a relief when morning comes and the light fills the room, putting my worries back in perspective.

Light helps us find the way.

Light always makes a difference, whether it's the gentle light of a candle or the bright light of a bulb.

Photocopying permitted under CLA Church Licence. Reproduced by permission from Bible Reading Fellowship.

Christmas is the time we celebrate that Jesus came to the earth to live among us. Jesus is called the 'light of the world' because he shows us that God loves us. He reassures us because he hears us when we talk to him, and he guides us through life.

We'd love to invite you to our Christmas services. *(Give local details.)*

We wish you all a very happy Christmas and we look forward to seeing you in the New Year when we start back on *(xx)* January.

May God bless you and all those you love this Christmas!

Mothering Sunday

Cast all your anxiety on him because he cares for you.
1 PETER 5:7

▶ **Watch:** 'The Mum Song' (**youtu.be/Nem0bkErGVY**)

This is a funny song and it makes me smile every time I watch it.

Being a parent or carer of small children (and actually children of any age) brings much joy but also much stress!

There are so many things to juggle every day. It is our job to keep them clean, warm, fed (and don't they always seem to be hungry!), stimulated, educated and cherished, while also managing all the other things we need to fit into each day.

Our verse today says, 'Cast all your anxiety on him [God] because he cares for you.' The Bible tells us that God loves us even more than we love our children! That is a hard concept to grasp for many of us. If we can absorb that truth, I think it will give us the strength we need as we care for our children.

Looking back over my experience of parenting three boys and running various parenting courses, I think there are a few things I would say to my younger self. Here are some of my top tips in parenting:

Focus on the good behaviour; give more attention to that and give less attention to bad behaviour.

Children need boundaries and feel most secure when they understand where those boundaries are. No must mean no!

Photocopying permitted under CLA Church Licence. Reproduced by permission from Bible Reading Fellowship.

Have fun together! Our children are with us for relatively short amount of time and although it is hard work, seemingly endless and can be pretty boring, one day they will have left home and we will look back and wonder where all those years went. Seize the day! Try to enjoy those small, boring moments. Don't rush too quickly on to the next stage because once it's gone, it's gone.

Invest in your relationship with your partner. A strong partnership is one of the best gifts you can give your children. *(You might want to signpost to courses such as The Marriage Course –* **themarriagecourse.org***.)*

Easter – sacrificial love

For God so loved the world that he gave his one and only Son, that whoever believes in him shall not perish but have eternal life.
JOHN 3:16

▶ **Watch:** *Frozen* clip where Olaf explains to Anna what real love is (**youtu.be/upzRUDLalIE**)

Olaf shows Anna what real love is. He demonstrates the sacrificial element of true love.

Easter is the time we remember God's sacrificial love for us.

We live in a broken world and God gave us his one and only Son, Jesus, so that our relationship with God could be restored. Despite all the ways we have turned our back on him and done things our own way and lived with 'I' at the centre (which the Bible calls 'sin'), God made a way for us to come back to him. He loves us and longs for us to know that love and to live life to the full.

God's gift of Jesus to us is:

- **personal** – he gave us his Son, offering redemption for where we have gone wrong.
- **practical** – it helps us to live new lives in his strength.
- **permanent/everlasting** – not **perishable** like so many of the material things around us that we treasure.

Happy Easter, everyone!

End of the summer term

Look after yourself first

[God says,] 'I will refresh the weary and satisfy the faint.'
JEREMIAH 31:25

▶ Watch: *Frozen* – 'In summer' (**youtu.be/UFatVn1hP3o**)

We've come to the end of term, and this is our final Refresh of the academic year. Some of you will be looking forward to the holiday, but many of you won't. Having eight weeks with your children without the routines, structures and punctuation of Refresh and the other groups you attend each week can feel like a long empty space stretching out in front of you.

I would really like to encourage you to connect with friends you have made here. Perhaps meet in a local park every Wednesday morning for those who are around.

We are mostly creatures of habit and need routine to mark our day, so put some in your schedule that will help you to pace yourself. Have a low-key plan in your mind, for example a walk in the morning, something else in the afternoon and have a little unstructured time to pause.

On aeroplanes, the safety demonstration always tells you to put the oxygen mask on yourself first, before putting it on the children. This struck me as odd when I heard it, because as a parent your first instinct is to protect your child before yourself. But as I thought about it, it really does make sense. In order to be able to protect our children, we need

Photocopying permitted under CLA Church Licence. Reproduced by permission from Bible Reading Fellowship.

to have enough oxygen ourselves. If we put the mask on our children first, we might not physically be able to help them at all. This is a useful metaphor for us as we think about the long holiday ahead. We need to make sure we put our oxygen mask on first, so we are at full capacity to deal with our children in the best possible way.

My question and encouragement to you is, 'What do you need to do each day in order that you are able to care for your children well?' and 'What is your metaphorical oxygen mask?'

Perhaps linger a little longer in the toilet (if you are alone in there!) and have those moments to pause and breathe slowly and deeply; arrange to meet a friend or someone you are just getting to know at Refresh; ask God to refresh you – I do that every day.

Think about what helps you – perhaps being outside, walking in the park in the fresh air enjoying nature and the beauty of creation. Perhaps reading your book in the bath after the children are in bed. Then try to weave these into your day.

Other ideas and tips

These could be done as interviews too.

- Yours or a team member's favourite verse and why
- Story of an answered prayer
- Story of a God-incidence
- The difference Alpha has made to an individual
- The difference (having a relationship with) God makes in your life
- What helps you when you are afraid?
- Tell the story (briefly) or quote from a Christian hero's life, for example Corrie Ten Boom

Top tips

- Keep it short – five minutes maximum!
- Use everyday language, not Christian jargon
- Be gentle
- Remember the aim is to introduce the adult guests to Jesus
- Speak from your personal experience
- In conversations with guests, follow their lead and be sensitive to their signals. Never push them to talk about spiritual matters if they don't want to.

Appendix 1

Refresh layout – diagrams of the setup

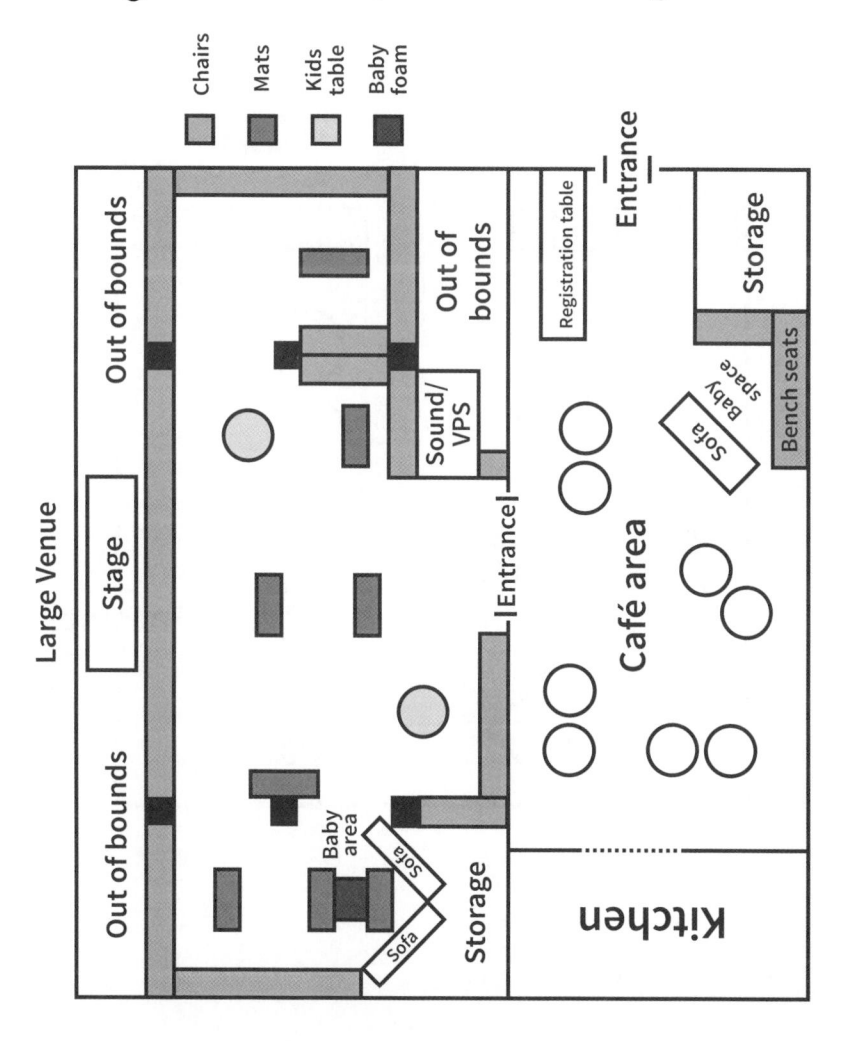

Small Venue

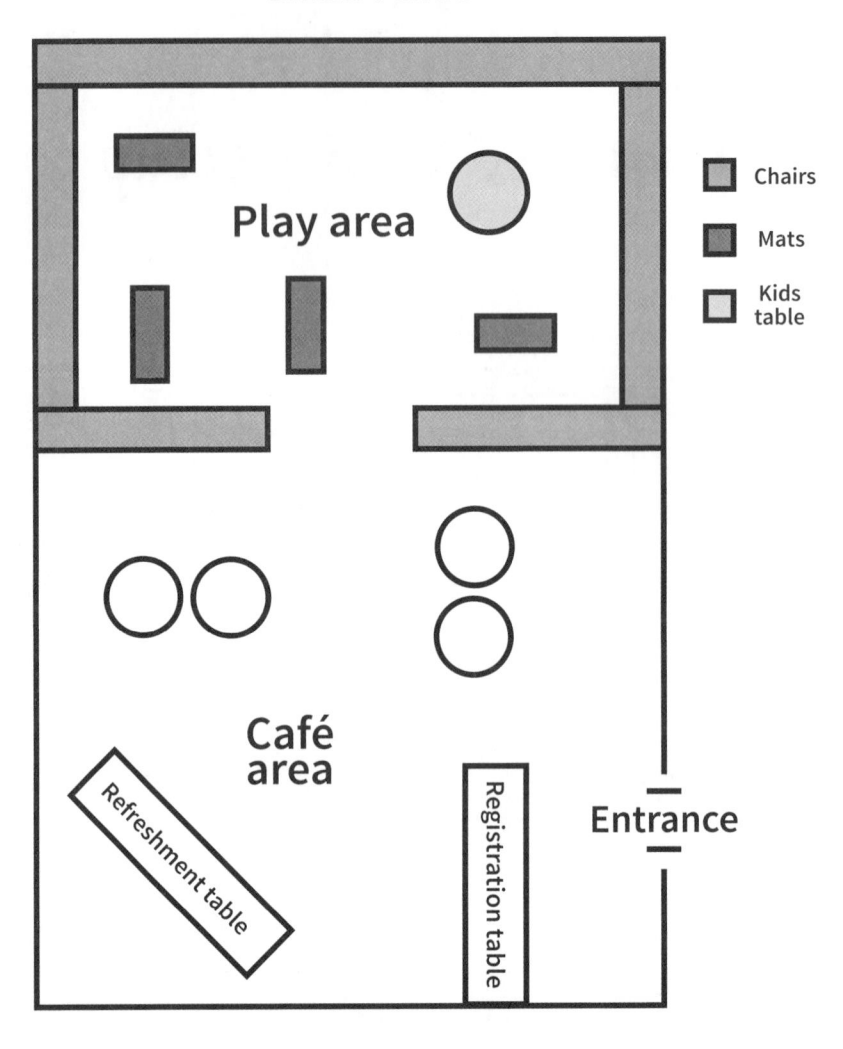

Play area

Café area

Refreshment table

Registration table

Entrance

- Chairs
- Mats
- Kids table

Appendix 2

Preparation to do in advance and on the day

In advance

- Buy the pastries and satsumas (keep the receipts if you need to claim back the money)
- Check that your church has milk (dairy and non-dairy), a variety of teas, coffee, biscuits, sugar, sweetener and squash
- Make the playdough (approximately every three weeks)
- Prepare the verse for the day and print off the required number (aim for one per adult guest)
- Check which team members are available
- Print some colouring sheets for the children (printable colouring pages are available on the internet)
- Check the registration book is ready (see example in Appendix 4)
- Check there are name stickers for the adults
- Check there are fun stickers for the children

On the day

- Set out the toys
- Set up the kitchen
- Set up the café area
- Set up the registration table

Appendix 3

List of toys we use and playdough recipe

- Small cars, a road mat and garage
- Duplo or Mega Bloks
- Books
- Magnets
- Train table with trains
- Dolls
- Play food
- Jigsaw puzzles
- Threading
- Dressing-up, including a doctor's kit
- Doll's house or Happyland
- Stickle Bricks or Noah's ark and animals
- Soft and hard baby toys
- Colouring table with colouring sheets (available online to download and print for free) and crayons
- Playdough table with playdough and playdough cutters

The playdough and colouring tables and chairs are child-sized.

We make the playdough (recipe below) because that is more economical and as it engages our sense of touch it feels very satisfying! We vary the colour we make, and everyone enjoys playing with it.

Playdough recipe

— Ingredients

480 g plain flour
480 g salt
90 ml (6 tablespoons) cream of tartar
45 ml (3 tablespoons) sunflower oil
750 ml boiling water
Food colouring

— Method

Mix all the dry ingredients together in a mixing bowl. Add the sunflower oil and boiling water and mix well.

Knead the mixture (careful: it's hot!). Adjust the texture by adding more water or flour accordingly.

Store in an airtight container once cooled.

Appendix 4

Registration table list and sample register

Registration table list

- Registration book to log names of guests and team (see sample below)
- Pens
- Name label stickers
- Blue and red sharpies to write the guests' names
- Children's smiley face stickers (or similar)
- Cash tin with a float (we have £30 – two £5 notes and the rest in £1 and £2 coins)
- Contactless payment machine if you have one
- Forms for guests to give contact details (voluntary but useful in case we are concerned about a child or if we need to cancel a session)
- Box of tissues
- Hand sanitiser
- Prayer request basket (with a lid) and a notebook and pen for guests to write their request on
- Notebook in case we need to note anything down

Sample register

This helps us to gauge the number of families and children that come each week and helps us remember their names.

No of families	Adult	Child
1	Jane	Max + Sophie
2	Chris + Elaine	Joe
3	Christine *	Harry + Katy
4		
5		
6		
7		

* we put a star next to any newcomers to give us an idea of how many there are each week

At the registration desk we give each adult a name sticker to help us get to know one another.

If they have been before, we write their name in blue. If they are new, we write their name in red. This helps the team identify who is new and they can keep a special lookout for them and introduce them to other people.

Appendix 5

Examples of Bible verses with pictures

> I will **refresh** the weary and **satisfy** the faint.
>
> *Jeremiah 31:25*

Image © Mathew Schwartz on Unsplash

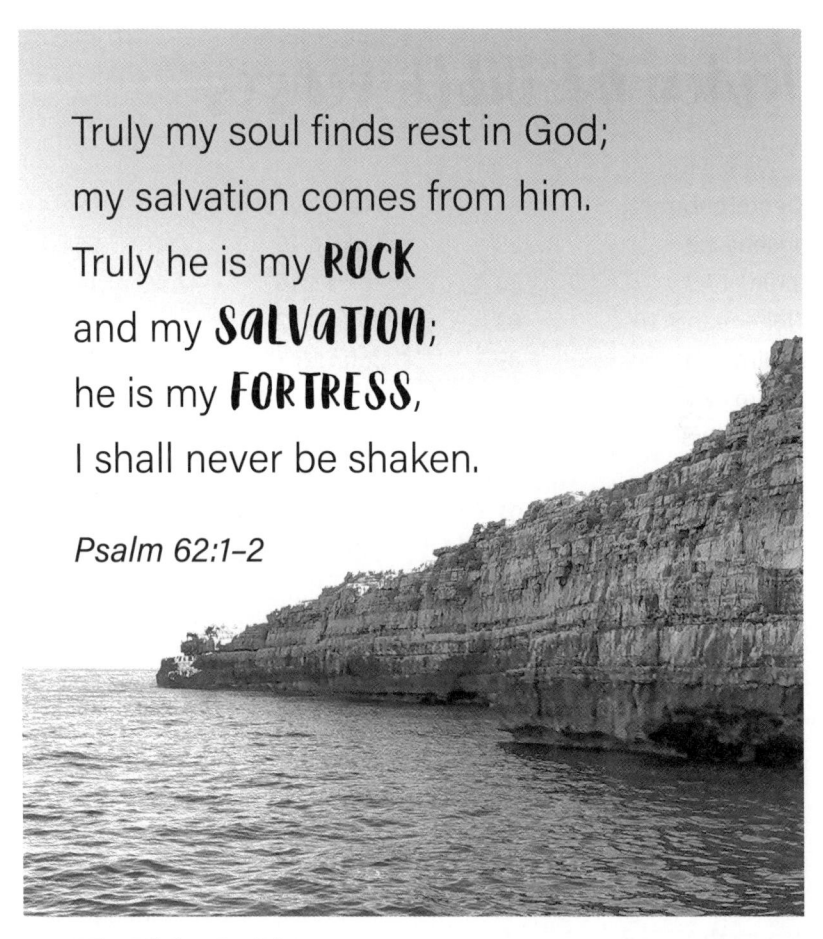

> Truly my soul finds rest in God;
> my salvation comes from him.
> Truly he is my **ROCK**
> and my **SALVATION**;
> he is my **FORTRESS**,
> I shall never be shaken.
>
> *Psalm 62:1–2*

Image © Thay Pellerin on Unsplash

Go to **brfonline.org.uk/refresh** to find all 30 Bible verse cards in colour for easy download and printing

Appendix 6

Index of Bible verses

Deuteronomy 23:5	85	Matthew 5:44–45	99
Joshua 1:9	23	Luke 6:45	95
2 Kings 7:9	13	John 3:16	111
Nehemiah 8:10	63	John 8:12	107
Psalm 46:1	89	John 13:34	40
Psalm 62:1–2	103	Romans 14:19	97
Psalm 62:8	61	Romans 15:13	105
Psalm 118:5	101	1 Corinthians 2:9	80
Psalm 118:6	91	1 Corinthians 12:12	70
Psalm 127:1-2	14	1 Corinthians 13:12	87
Psalm 139:1–2	83	Ephesians 4:32	98
Psalm 139:13–14	78, 81	Philippians 4:6–7	59
Psalm 145:18	72	1 Peter 5:7	109
Ecclesiastes 3:1	75	1 John 3:1	88
Isaiah 40:31	93		
Isaiah 43:18–19	69		
Isaiah 55:1	13		
Isaiah 58:11	73		
Isaiah 61:1-3	13		
Jeremiah 17:7–8	65		
Jeremiah 31:25	13, 76, 96, 112		
Jeremiah 33:3	67		

God makes us the most unbelievable offer... to be our parent. Yes, even when we're all grown up and have children of our own! But many of us don't live experiencing the connection, guidance and support that's on offer. Why? Because we've forgotten how to be a child. In this easy-to-read guide, Anna Hawken explores ten different ways to rediscover our 'child side'. She uses the living, breathing examples of the children in our lives to inspire and challenge us, by looking at things that we sometimes struggle with but they are great at. Read it on your own or with others, using the individual reflections, questions and small group notes to guide you. These simple ideas will help even the busiest parent to draw closer to God.

Being God's Child: A Parent's Guide
Ten things you can learn from your kids
Anna Hawken
978 1 80039 198 7 £6.99

brf.org.uk

Our children's early years are incredibly significant in shaping their mental, emotional and spiritual lives for the future, but how do we sow seeds of faith when they are so tiny? In this book Rachel Turner suggests simple, everyday approaches to help our children connect with the God who knows them. Wherever you are on your faith journey, you can help your child meet and know God, and however young your child is, God loves them and has promises for them.

Babies and Toddlers
Nurturing your child's spiritual life
Rachel Turner
978 1 80039 000 3 £4.99

brf.org.uk

A comprehensive foundation for those working in the increasingly complex and diverse area of ministry with families, *The Essential Guide to Family Ministry* presents an overview of contemporary family life, sets out the principles that underpin this work and offers strategic and practical approaches to working with families. An essential read for all who are involved in this field and passionate about seeing God's kingdom come in families, churches and communities.

The Essential Guide to Family Ministry
A practical guide for church-based family workers
Gail Adcock
978 0 85746 578 8   £8.99

brf.org.uk

BRF *Enabling all ages to grow in faith*

Anna Chaplaincy
Living Faith
Messy Church
Parenting for Faith

BRF is a Christian charity that resources individuals and churches. Our vision is to enable people of all ages to grow in faith and understanding of the Bible and to see more people equipped to exercise their gifts in leadership and ministry.

To find out more about our work, visit

brf.org.uk